It Was Not Your Fault
How to Overcome the Negative Effects of Childhood Sexual Abuse.

BY

LINDSEY LISH PREECE

Expl☉ra
B O O K S

EXPLORA BOOKS
700 – 838 West Hastings St. Vancouver, BC V6C 0A6
www.explorabooks.com
Phone: (604) 330 6795

ISBN: 978-1-998394-35-7(eBook)
978-1-998394-34-0 (Paperback)

LINDSEY LISH PREECE

IT WAS NOT YOUR FAULT

HOW TO OVERCOME THE NEGATIVE EFFECTS OF CHILDHOOD SEXUAL ABUSE

Book Testimonials

The things I've told myself for years inside my head were very negative and I had a lot of fear. After reading Lindsey's book, I had to really think abt (and catch myself) in these lies. Boy was this an eye opening exercise! Now after implementing one of the exercises consistently…I'm starting to feel the shift. Thankful for being able to find this book and start working on a much more positive mindset that will help to elevate me instead of keeping me in a rut. Thanks again Lindsey for your help in turning this around for me.

-Colie Pate-Price-

I am seeing a lot of progress after implementing the tools in this book. I am genuinely liking myself again, the amount of negativity in my head is minimal compared to what it was before, and when it does creep in –I know how to snap out much quicker and catch myself. When traumatic things happen, I've got actual tools to help me process it in a healthy way. The tools are GOLD and I am forever thankful for God bringing this book into my life when He did.

-Tammy Harvey-

I've only practiced the first tool Lindsey shares in this book and I am so pleased. I've never liked affirmations, but she gives them purpose and I was able to use them in a new way. They helped me feel good about myself! They made me smile! They gave me confidence! They gave me a sense of self worth! Affirmations never meant anything to me and now they do! They are a blessing to my life. I am so grateful for what I have learned! It has made my outlook on life better than it was before.

-Jillian Bitter-

I feel really proud and content with myself. We just experienced our second pipe flooding in 5 years. The first time it happened, I was completely overwhelmed and felt like our lives were falling apart. It felt like "déjà vu," last week, but this time was more challenging, because my husband was out of town, leaving me to handle everything on my own. Despite the familiar feelings that resurfaced, I quickly remembered the strategies I've learned and have been practicing regularly from Lindsey's book and teaching. Implementing these techniques, I was pleasantly surprised that I remained calm, composed, and communicated promptly and respectfully with everyone involved. Despite the tough situation, I didn't feel defeated in the end. I actually feel confident in my progress and optimistic about the future with this new perspective on my life and myself. Thank you for writing this book Lindsey!

-Shana Albrecht-

It Was Not Your Fault

How to Overcome the Negative Effects of Childhood Sexual Abuse.

Table of Contents

INTRODUCTION

Hi! I am so glad you are here!

This is my big introduction to help you decide why you should read this book! My name is Lindsey Lish Preece and this book is about my unfortunate story of childhood sexual abuse, the many lies I was living thereafter, and how I was able to overcome the negative effects of the abuse.

One thing I know for sure is the abuse wasn't my fault and it wasn't your fault, but I didn't always believe that. I know many girls and women live years of blaming themselves after experiencing such painful events and this one lie can keep us from living our lives to their full potential. I believe life was made to have joy every single day amidst the storms and it is so important for us to figure out how to find that joy. On the flip side, if we continue to believe the abuse was our fault, detrimental life choices can creep into our worlds, causing much unnecessary suffering.

I wrote this book, to share how I discovered this lie, how I overcame it (along with many other lies and detrimental effects of the abuse), and to offer hope and di-rection to you along your road to recovery from child-hood sexual abuse. My hope is that you can learn some-thing from my story that may set you free from the bondage you are in and open your mind to the fact that a beautiful life is absolutely possible after abuse. Are you tired of the painful memories of your abuse showing up again and again? Do you feel shame, anger, worthless-ness, fear, etc. related to the abuse? Have you ever felt that your life is over? Or worthless? Have you ever believed that you deserved the abuse? That you'll never get over it? Or that you will never amount to anything now? Then this book is for you.

If you answered yes to any of the above questions, please know that these are all lies that you have been living possibly for years. They have been playing so loudly in your mind that you have accepted them as truth. You may not even recognize them as there, or they may be ruining your life. Either way, it is time to identify them and get rid of them forever!

The most important takeaways I hope you get from this book are: Knowing and believing the abuse was not your fault, happiness every single day and a beautiful, bright future is definitely possible, forgiveness is achievable, and you are simply amazing just the way you are today! All of these takeaways are 100% up to you! But don't worry, I will show you why and how to get there. So, are you ready for positive change? Let's get to it!

But first, I'm sure you want to know who in the world I am and why you should trust me. So, here's a little introduction:

It Was Not
Your Fault
How to Overcome the Negative
Effects of Childhood Sexual Abuse.

CHAPTER 1

MY STORY

I was born and raised in Tremonton, Utah to a wonderful mother and father. My family was very well known in our little community and we were a church-going family. I had an older sister and younger brother. We fought like most kids, but also played a lot together with neighbor kids in the alfalfa fields behind our house and on the dirt hills.

As a little girl, I was a daddy's girl. I loved my dad, and my favorite time of day was when I would hear his truck pull into the driveway, meaning he was done with work for the day. I would run out to the garage and greet him and then spend the rest of the evening following him around as he finished his chores. We had many animals to feed, a huge garden and fruit trees to attend to, and a large, beautiful yard to upkeep. Among the hundreds of animals (chickens, ducks, rabbits, salamanders, dogs, a turtle, chipmunks) were bobcats. Dad trapped them as a hobby and decided one day it would be fun to have them as pets. We bottle-fed them from birth, and they were declawed so we could interact with them. Our home was often a spot for school field trips. Who needs to travel to the zoo when you can walk to Lindsey's house? That was one of my favorite childhood memories.

I wanted to be just like my dad and one of my biggest goals was to do whatever I needed to hear my dad say how proud he was of me. I got that satisfaction many times a year as I bounced through the door to share my report card with him. He would always say, "You are so smart Lindsey girl, and I am so proud of you." That was all the motivation I needed to continue getting straight A's throughout my school career.

Dad was a diesel truck driver and I loved taking my turn going to work with him and riding in his big, red truck and talking on the CB to his truck driver brothers and friends. I was known as "dancer," to all of them, and I loved it.

One year my dad sectioned off a piece of our garden just for me to grow and care for my very own plants and vegetables. This was the highlight of that summer and I still love growing a garden every year.

My dad loved the Utah Jazz, so I did too. We would share many evenings eating saltine crackers smothered in butter with a tall glass of milk as we cheered for Mark Eaton, Thurle Bailey, John Stockton, and Karl Malone. What fun memories!

Mom was my role model. She worked outside of our home at Grandpa Lowell's gas station to help make ends meet. She loved her job and all the friendships she had made at work. Mom cooked a perfect meal every night for dinner and we would all sit around our huge oak table and laugh as we ate.

Mom was full of kindness and love for others, and everyone knew her as the sweetest lady around. She was always laughing. Everything was funny to her. If I was with mom, I never had to laugh, she did it for both of us.

Mom knew what she believed and shared that freely with us children. I never wondered what was in her heart, because she would express it. All of the good at least. I never remember hearing a negative word come out of her mouth. My favorite memory of her was seeing her kneeling at her bed every single night saying her prayers for what seemed like hours. How could she talk to God for that long? What in the world did she have to say?

I loved being home because it was a safe place for me. Mom always played her favorite spiritual music that I found comforting, especially after a tough day with friends at school. Mom loved me and I knew it. She never picked favorites, we were all treated equally, and I loved that.

I loved school. I enjoyed learning, especially Science and Math, but mostly loved spending time with friends. I was not the quiet type. I wore my feelings on my sleeve and said exactly what was on my mind. I was never afraid of standing up for what I thought was true or summoning a teacher when a fight broke out. To some, this was a characteristic they wished they had, but to others, it was annoying and overbearing. Because of this, I was often blamed for any wrongdoings of my friend group and known as the one in charge. I hated always being blamed, but I can see clearly why now. My friend group was known as "Lindsey's group."

I was bossy and got along with boys better than girls. I never really had a best friend, and that was difficult. But I was surrounded by cousins, family, and a group of girls that were kind to me (bless their hearts). I grew up loving people and enjoyed being in charge. I had great self-esteem, and nothing was going to stop me from creating an amazing future.

Then everything changed. When I was 12 years old, at a sleepover, I was sexually abused while I was asleep. It awoke me and I remember turning and watching some-one run out of the room. The next morning, I was con-fused as I recalled what had happened. "Please tell me that was a dream," I remember thinking. I asked the other girl that was in the room and she said the same thing happened to her. I immediately rehearsed the story to my mom and because a male sibling was sleep-ing on the floor, we concluded it must have been him. We confronted the 8-year-old boy and he cried and ex-claimed, "I would never do something like that." We left it alone.

As time went on, I realized who my abuser was. I told mom and she confronted the person we will call Bob, and he surprisingly admitted to the abuse. I was devastated! My life started crumbling all around me. Bob was someone I was close to, had spent a lot of time with, completely trusted, and grew to love. Why would he do this to me? To my family? He was ripped out of my life very soon after that and taken to jail.

The anger and confusion felt intense. The main memories I had after that day were constant, intense feelings of anger and confusion. I would spend hours crying in my bed, pounding my fist on the floor and trying to figure out how I could make all of this go away.

From that day forward, I struggled to sleep at night, I felt strong feelings of depression and anxiety, the fear was debilitating, and survival was my goal for each day. Even though Bob was now in jail, I was petrified he would get out soon and he would do it again.

My mom was amazing. She believed me from day one and I remember her saying her top priority was my safety. That was comforting. She got me into counseling right away. I was so angry! "Counseling is for crazy people, and I'm not crazy (even though deep down I wondered)!" I told her. I hated the first couple of therapists and then finally, we found the perfect fit. I quickly shifted from fighting my mom and crying each week on the way to counseling, to not being able to wait for Tuesdays when I could see my therapist. The relief I would feel as I left that building each week was priceless. I was given the ability to cope and survive another week the best that I knew how. But, come Sunday I was praying for Tuesday to arrive as soon as possible so I could relax on that couch and unload everything out of my head. I believe counseling saved me.

Living in a small town and being a well-known family isn't always a good thing. Eventually, everyone knew what had happened and going back to school and church was humiliating. I still remember little gifts friends gave me in an attempt to let me know they cared. I just wished no one knew about it. I heard comments like, "Wow, I never thought something like this would happen to you." As if that was supposed to make it any better.

Then, comments from a few particular people caused the beginnings of self-blame. The shame was debilitating. I don't even know how I continued going to school and living my life. I soon found myself in a doctor's office starting on antidepressants to help me cope. It did help take the edge off, and the constant crying became controllable.

One of the earliest activities I remember my therapist encouraging me to do was to keep a notebook handy and each time I felt the anger peering, to scribble all of the yuck out of my head and onto paper. That speedily became a multiple-time-a-day activity. The anger was intense and oftentimes all I could focus on was how I could make sure Bob was feeling the pain he had caused in me, and to understand why he had so willingly ruined my life. With advice from my therapist, this writing soon developed into letters to Bob. I wrote everything and held nothing back! It felt so good to tell him exactly what was on my mind, and I hoped he was hurting just like me. And then, I had my mom send Bob every single letter.

As time went by and I had faithfully expressed my anger in every possible way, it started subsiding. Some of the anger slowly turned into compassion. I remembered from the moment my mom confronted Bob, he admit-ted what he had done and expressed the need for help. He never blamed me and took full responsibility. I don't remember if my mom told me or if it came from Bob, but I was told he was very sorry for what he had done, and he was seeking help. He started counseling of his own and I remember hearing he was having a very difficult time and felt great remorse for what he had done to me and my family. As angry as I still was with him, I noticed a shift. It was now ok for me to say anything and everything damaging about Bob that came to mind, but as soon as others defamed him, I would get very defensive and angry, and I wanted to defend him.

The anger, resentment, and defensiveness continued for years as I grew into a young adult. Some of the most difficult were my teenage years. I ached for a replacement for Bob in my life. I hated seeing relationships friends had with influential men. I was jealous to see the support they had throughout all of their accomplishments and activities in high school and college. I craved validation and found that in constant relationships. Time did begin to heal my wounds with Bob, but new aftereffects, I didn't see coming, soon became very ap-parent. I did my best to stuff them away hoping they would just disappear.

When I got married, I felt ready, so I invited Bob to the wedding. It was obvious many family members did not approve, but I did not want Bob to miss out on any more of my life. I had opened up and shared my story with my new husband and he was nothing short of amazing. He trusted that I was ready and loved and accepted Bob for who he had become. To this day I have never heard a harsh word towards him. That doesn't mean we don't have boundaries and are oblivious to the fact that it could happen again, but because of our situation, we have chosen to forgive and include Bob in our lives.

I would be lying if I said I haven't had any issues related to the abuse in my adulthood. It is crazy how something painful many years earlier can continue to negatively affect you for years to come. In my own relationships and raising my own little family, I have faced many difficulties that have been identified as aftereffects of the abuse with the help of professionals. I will discuss these in this book as well.

It has now been almost 20 years since the abuse, and I am so relieved to say I have a wonderful relationship with Bob. He has worked very hard over the last 20 years to become someone new. I know many of you reading this won't ever have the opportunity to hear your abuser say sorry or admit to the abuse at all. You may never have the chance to talk with them or repair your relationship and that is completely ok. I can tell you if that had been the case for me, I would have still searched anywhere and everywhere to find healing for myself and it would have come in the exact same form that I will be sharing with you in this book. You don't have to have specific details to your story to find healing and happiness. It will all come from what you choose to do for YOU!! And a relationship with your abuser does not need to be a part of that. In fact, in many situations, a relationship would make things much more difficult. I will explain.

My Family Today

I have been very fortunate to birth three beautiful girls. I never dreamed I would ever get the chance to raise just one, so when three came I was thrilled! Our girls are each very different, and I love each one for their silly quirks and beautiful gifts. Irelynd is sensitive, full of fun, always caring for others and has her head on straight! Oftentimes the wise perspective that comes out of her mouth shocks the heck out of me! Kynlee is full of giggles, my right-hand housemaid, and hanging with friends is a top priority. Watching the development of her shyness into more solid self-confidence has caused my mommy heart to swell. Bentlee is my mini-me. "In-dependent" and "Stubborn" are her middle names, at home at least. She is one we get a call on weekly from teachers and principals expressing their gratitude for the kind and thoughtful character she is. She has a heart of gold and it shines through her actions.

Jared, my husband, is a tall, dark and handsome, greenish-blue-eyed hunk and he is the perfect fit for me. I'm not kidding when I say this, it freaks me right out thinking of how my own immature stupidity almost lost him in my college years. I always thought he was too good to be true, and after 20 years of marriage, I am still con-fused as heck at how I landed him. He serves his girls from a silver platter and they have him wrapped around their fingers. Although deep down I'm sure he would have loved to have his own sports-loving son, I have never heard a word of it from his mouth. He dreams about snowmobiling year-round and loves to explore the world hand in hand. If given the chance, I would marry him over and over again, but maybe erase some of the turmoil and grief I put him through in our dating years.

I have been a Registered Nurse with a Bachelors' degree for 19 years and my passion has always been to im-prove the lives of others and encouraging them to reach for the stars! I attempted my Master's degree in Nursing and was quickly deterred down a path of serving women. About 2 years ago I had a thought that freaked me right out! "You need to share your personal story of sexual abuse, healing, forgiveness and how you are now living a happy and joyful life." What? Me? Why? Where did that thought come from?

At that time, I was working with women in an online challenge system, focusing on their holistic health. I ignorantly became aware of the vast population of women suffering from what I had personally defeated (the after-effects of childhood sexual abuse). Many expressed the desire for help, but unsure of where to turn or who to trust to guide them. I knew it was time to share my story in an attempt to fill any part of this void. I developed a Facebook and Instagram page entitled *itwasnotyourfault*, just finished this book sharing all the details of my story, and I will be starting a podcast very soon walking through my experience and the specific tactics that led to my healing.

Now let's dive into the details that truly changed my heart and mind over time and lead me to forgiveness and an abundant life filled with happiness.

CHAPTER 2

STAGES OF HEALING (GRIEF)

For a long time, I remember praying I would just wake up and this nightmare of a life I was living would be back to normal. I tried convincing myself it was not reality, and I was just living a dream I would soon awake from.

Well, the reality of the abuse never vanished, so I was left to continue in misery or figure some way out! And that's exactly what I started doing, with the guidance of many professionals as a young girl, as well as in my adulthood. So where did I begin and where do we begin?

There is definitely a process to healing after childhood sexual abuse, and I found that the 5 stages of grief and loss discovered by a Swiss-American psychiatrist named Elizabeth Kübler-Ross explain the process well. These stages include denial, anger, bargaining, depression, and acceptance. Not everyone will go through every stage, and the stages can be experienced in any particular order.[1] Let's first discuss denial.

Oftentimes, victims of childhood sexual abuse will convince themself that part or parts of their real story didn't happen, in an attempt to be able to function after the abuse. Sometimes the facts are so debilitating that a conscious decision is made to erase the memories altogether. Many victims eventually become unsure of the actual truth of their story, because they have suppressed the event/s or believed the cover up story for so long. Without fail, sometime in the future, the victim will encounter an event that will bring up the horrifying memories forcing either acknowledgment and acceptance or continued repression.

For example, I have a friend who as a young girl was sexually abused repetitively by a neighbor. She had completely forgotten these events. When she got married, sexual intercourse with her new husband brought back all of the memories. She was overcome with confusion and anxiety as she tried to sort through all of the emotions and details flooding her mind. She attended counseling and was assisted through processing, acknowledging and accepting very painful details about her abuse. It has taken work, but she is well on her way to overcoming.

1 Theo, "The Five Stages Of Grief."

Our minds are so powerful. Isn't it amazing that our brains have the ability to erase or disguise anything that could cause us emotional harm? If this has happened to you, just know that you did nothing wrong and were doing your best to protect yourself without even recognizing it. The best thing you can do now is work to-wards acknowledging, accepting, and overcoming. It is completely possible, and I will show you how.

As a young girl, I was an avid daily journal writer. A few months ago, I opened my journal curious to see what I had recorded about the abuse. I combed through the months before and after. I was shocked. I recognized I had a period of denial as well. I didn't see it then as such and I wonder if I just didn't want to remember the details in the future, or it was just too painful to write about, but there was very little written about the abuse or any of the circumstances surrounding it. Either way, there was definitely a stage of denial and not wanting to accept it as my reality.

In the last year or so when reading Journey to Heal, I was educated on the why behind the importance of accepting and acknowledging the abuse as an actual part of a victims' life. Until you are able to accept and acknowledge the abuse, you will not be able to begin the process of complete healing.[2] I thought back to my childhood and recognized that this acceptance came a few years after the abuse. I remember not wanting to accept it, because I felt that meant I was broken, or something was wrong with me. I eventually recognized as I accepted the abuse as part of my story, the burden I was carrying became lighter and my desire for this new-found freedom became stronger.

But what if I don't want to accept it? Are there other negative effects? Again, I learned in my reading, repressing anger or denying parts of your story can be very dangerous to the victim long term. Various aftereffects naturally occur following traumatic experiences such as sexual abuse, if any part of the incident/s is not accepted or acknowledged.

What? Aftereffects? I was intrigued. How much of who I am today stems from the abuse? As I continued reading, I was baffled to note that almost every characteristic noted was me to a T. At least issues I had dealt with for the last 30 years. Some of those included perfectionism, need to control anyone and everything around me, anxiety, depression, overeating, eating disorders, body im-age issues, irrational insecurities, feeling irritated and impatient especially with my close family members, an-ger issues, and having a difficult time showing love to others. Wow! I finally had the answer to the question I had been asking myself for years, "What is wrong with me?"

2 Sutherland, *Journey to Heal*.

3 Sutherland.

Please tell me I am not alone. Can any of you relate? My conclusion after some much-needed guidance from a close friend, Kimberly Watts, and life coach of 15 plus years: *"Nothing is wrong with you, you have endured a traumatic childhood experience and your reactions are the result. It's time to recognize, not blame, take responsibility, and start working on ridding yourself of each and every one, so you can become the very best version of you."* What beautiful advice. Further I learned, if left unresolved, these aftereffects could lead to destructive behaviors such as drug use and addiction, heavy drinking, promiscuity and sexual addictions, cut-ting and harming oneself, and compulsive spending are just a few. Rehab centers, homeless shelters, addiction recovery facilities, hospitals, counseling offices, and prisons everywhere are filled with men and women who were sexually abused as children (and never dealt with the abuse effectively) and are now suffering the effects of that abuse in a profound way.[4]

If you have found some of this or all of it resonate with you, don't worry, it's not too late. But it is time to ad-dress these issues from the inside out. Are you ready? I'll teach you some specific tactics in the next section.

Stage #1: Acknowledging and Accepting the Abuse

As explained above, acknowledging the truth of your story and accepting it as part of your life is paramount to the beginning stages of healing. I learned this first technique from the book Journey to Heal and found tremendous results for myself after following. Fair warning, you might find this part painful, and that is not only ok, but expected. Take your time to get through each exercise, it is not a race. Remember, the outcome will be so worth it!

Start by writing all the details of your story as you know them to be true. Write EVERYTHING, leaving nothing out. Here are a couple of questions from the Journey to Heal author that helped me and can help you write your story as well:

How old were you when the abuse began?

Who was involved?

What happened?

Was it a one-time event, or was it repeated over time?

Write until you cannot remember anything more.

4 Sutherland, 40.

Next, read through what you have written consciously accepting that this is your real story and an actual part of your life. Remember, it is ok to be flooded with emotions. Work through them as you need, take your time, this is not a race. Once you are finished writing, you can decide what to do with it: burn it, rip it up, or save it, etc. Whatever you choose to do, as you are doing it, think about accepting it and letting all of it go.

Step by Step

1. Write all the details of your story as you remember them.

   - How old were you when the abuse started?
   - Who was involved?
   - What happened?

2. Was it a one-time event, or was it repeated over time? Read

back through what you have written, consciously accepting the details as part of your story.

3. Burn it, rip it up, or save it.

You did it! How do you feel? If you feel some relief, great! If you feel terrible, that is great too! You are working through the pain so you can let it go. You may have to repeat this more than once to get the desired effect. Major change will not happen overnight, but you will notice subtle changes right away. Don't stop! You are on your way to a bright and beautiful future. Trust me.

Stage #2 Anger

Let's talk about anger. Have you ever felt or maybe still feel that if you just open your mouth, you are sure you could spit fire? I had so much heaviness in my chest that I carried every day for a very long time. I truly felt I wanted to scream from the rooftops in an attempt to release all of the heat and pain. It was the last thing on my mind at night and the first thing I thought of when I opened my eyes in the morning. It was crippling! Can you relate?

When discussing anger after abuse, author Jackson Mackenzie educates, *"Anger is usually perceived as a "bad" emotion. You may have been taught not to talk about it or even acknowledge it. You may have been taught to stuff it down into the depths of you and/or force yourself to "let it go"—or at least,* say *that you have let it go—even though it is still festering inside you. But these are ineffective approaches to anger. It will find a way to torment you if you do not allow yourself to feel it, if you ignore it in one way or another, or if you pretend to let it go before you are ready. The truth is that anger is not "bad." When channeled appropriately, it has the potential to motivate all of us normal human beings to better ourselves, and it even has the potential to protect us from dangerous situations."* [5]

Anger is NOT bad!! Anger is a NORMAL reaction, especially after a traumatic experience. If you feel like yelling, yell. If you feel like punching something, punch a pillow. If you feel like killing someone, reach out for professional help! Author Jackson Mackenzie continues teaching, *"Ultimately, after you've experienced many waves of anger (less intense each time), and after you've found multiple ways to express it safely, and after you've determined that enough time has passed, you can make the conscious choice to let the rage go. There is no timeline for how long the anger should last."* [6]

5 MacKenzie, *Psychopath Free (Expanded Edition)*

The important truth is if you don't want the anger to continue showing up for the rest of your life, possibly causing you and those around you much more harm than good, then you need to learn how to deal with it appropriately. There are many creative ways to deal with anger including physical exercise, dance, art, storytelling, writing, cooking, creating something, etc.

Now if you are ready, it's your turn. Here are a few writing exercises that worked miracles for me! I also learned this one from the book, Journey to Heal. It is intended to help you begin dealing with and releasing the ineffective anger.

Step by Step
1. Acknowledge and accept that you have anger.
2. Ask yourself: If I could identify one thing about the abuse that hurts the most, what would it be?
3. Fill out this sentence with each person identified:

— I am angry with _____ because of _____

4. Expand upon each sentence you wrote for each person.

5. Write a letter to each of the people you wrote about on step

6. Rip it up, burn it, hide it, or send it.

First step, acknowledge the anger. Accept that you have anger or repressed anger that needs to be released. If you are not sure if you have anger to release, ask someone close to you if they see anger in you or feel you are holding onto anger. Be prepared to accept what they tell you and remember, you asked them. They just want to help you.

6 MacKenzie.

Next, ask yourself:

If I could identify one thing about the abuse that hurts the most, what would that be?

Does it have to do with your abuser, or someone indirectly involved, or with the abuse itself? (example of someone indirectly involved would be: You confided in your aunt and she didn't believe you or said you were lying or making it up for attention, and now you are angry with her.)

With each person identified, fill out this sentence:

I am angry with _____ because of _____

Remember my cute friend and life coach Kimberly Watts that gave me such great advice in the last chapter? This next part I learned from her:

Take each sentence you wrote in the last exercise and expand upon them. Write everything that is weighing you down or causing you feelings of anger about that person. Don't stop writing until you can't think of any-thing more. Do this for each person. Then set them aside. We'll come back to them in a minute or so.

I don't remember my counselors' face or name, but I will never forget one exercise she gave me that helped me to release the anger, without spitting fire of course. She explained that every time I felt anger building up inside, I was to take out a piece of paper and write a letter to the person I was thinking about. She told me to express all that I was feeling and not to hold back anything. I remember sitting day after day at our large, oak, kitchen table with a piece of paper in front of me and a pencil in hand scribbling down all of my thoughts and feelings as fast as I could possibly go. I'm sure I had a furrowed brow and appeared as if I was jotting down a plan to kill someone. Oh, it felt so good. Sometimes I did this multiple times a day, and oftentimes those letters took up pages and pages. Then, she told me, when you are finished, you can decide if you want to rip it up, burn it, hide it, or send it. I had my mom send every last letter! The satisfaction I felt from thinking Bob must be hurting like I was, was liberating.

Now it's your turn again. Take each of those sentences you have expanded upon and write a letter to the person you have anger towards. Include all the details of how you feel and how that person has negatively affected your life. Be honest, get all real feelings out of your head and onto paper. Write all the things that you would say if you had the courage to say them. Then rip it up, burn it, or send it.

Now I want to make something clear, just because I sent my letters does not mean you need to do the same. Any of the options (rip it up, burn it, hide it, or send it) will give you the same result. It's getting those feelings out of your head that begins the process of releasing the anger.

P.S. As a side note, I talked to Bob a couple of weeks ago about the letters, and he said he kept and still has every single one. I don't know if I ever want to read those letters again, for fear of experiencing that darkness and pain all over, but they sure served their purpose for the time being. My hope for you is that you feel the same way after completing these exercises.

I challenge you, for the next week, that each time you feel any type of anger, take out a paper or type up a letter expressing all of your feelings without holding back. Do it over and over and over again and then de-cide what you want to do with them each time you are finished. Then, at the end of the week evaluate how you feel. I can't wait to hear about it.

Stage #3: Bargaining

I love what MacKenzie had to say on this subject, *"During grief, you may feel vulnerable and helpless. In those moments of intense emotions, it's not uncommon to look for ways to regain control or to want to feel like you can affect the outcome of an event. In the bargaining stage of grief, you may find yourself creating a lot of "what if" and "if only" statements."*[7]

I can totally relate! I remember for quite a while after the abuse trying to figure out ways around the pain and wondering if it was possible to trick myself somehow so it wouldn't feel so painful. I wondered if hypnotism would help, if there was some kind of drug to erase my memory, and at times I even thought about how amazing it would be if I somehow slipped away in my sleep and didn't wake up the next morning. I also remember having very serious conversations with God. I would promise Him over and over that I would do anything He wanted if He would just take the pain away and make it all disappear. As time went by, and nothing changed, I grudgingly concluded I had to do the work.

7 MacKenzi

My conclusion, the memories of the abuse are never going to go away on their own, and it is a waste of time trying to figure out a way around the difficult parts of recovery. I knew, no matter how much it hurt, I had to push straight through it if I ever wanted to come out on the other side. But what I didn't expect was the immediate small amounts of relief I started feeling with every effort I put towards recovery. With each exercise, I would feel a small amount of the weight lift and it continued to get lighter and lighter the more determined and faithful I was to practice the tactics I was given. This is when I learned the power of consistency and sticking things out to the end.

Stage #4: Depression

Depression is real and a very common response to sexual abuse. For me, the depression sunk in when I recognized the abuse was never going to go away. I felt over-whelmed thinking of all the work it was going to take to push straight through. For a period of time, I didn't want to do what I thought it was going to take. I cried and cried and was miserable and withdrawn. I would sleep every chance I could, my motivation for life was poor, I wondered and asked why this had to happen to me, and I just didn't care much about what normally would have had me in knots.

When I was a young girl, the depression was lessened with medication. As an adult, about 2-3 years ago, I recognized I had lingering almost daily depression. Many of the tactics, especially the truths and lies activity I shared with you in this book would pull me out of it. I have also found daily exercise takes that sadness away. Getting out and being around people makes a huge difference and filling my mind with positivity lifts my spirit immensely.

CHAPTER 3

UNDERSTANDING AND BELIEVING IT WAS NOT YOUR FAULT!

A fter the abuse happened, I remember hearing that some acquaintances were implying that the abuse was my fault. They had said that something I did caused my perpetrator to abuse me. Until that day, that thought had never crossed my mind and I began wondering if I could have prevented the abuse and maybe it was my fault.

I don't believe Bob or anyone else blamed me. In fact, I remember my mom telling me that Bob admitted to the abuse right away and expressed HIS need for help. But I began to fear, was part of it my fault? I wondered and worried about this for a couple of years. Thanks to my educated counselor, I was able to dismiss this dam-aging lie within a couple years. As an adult, I have learned much more about this topic. When a child or anyone is sexually abused, whose fault is it? Well, let's examine that.

First and foremost, what exactly is sexual abuse? Dr. Dan Allender, a licensed psychologist whose specialty is sexual abuse recovery educates, *"Sexual abuse is any type of non-consensual sexual contact (to be consensual it has to be capable, informed, and unforced consent). This form of assault and abuse can happen to men or women of any age. Childhood sexual abuse is any con-tact or interaction (visual, verbal, or psychological) be-tween a child or adolescent and an adult when the child or adolescent is being used for the sexual stimulation of the perpetrator or any other person. Sexual abuse may be committed by a person under the age of eighteen when that person is either significantly older than the victim or in a position of power/control over the child/adolescent."* [8]

Once I understood this definition from a professional, I knew my conclusion of it not being my fault was correct. But did my naive and immature actions cause the abuse to happen? It is obvious that an adult can have absolute power over a child, but can a child have power over an adult? Did I have that type of power and control at such a young age, to cause someone else to act?

8 Sutherland, *Journey to Heal*, 34.

The answer is simple, *"You were powerless against your perpetrator."* [9] You were an innocent child, even if you were a teenager. Crystal M. Sutherland helps us to understand this by explaining that seeing herself in a photo album as a young girl at the age the abuse happened, helped her to remember and visually see her innocence. As I pulled out old journals and began reading before, during and after the time period of my abuse, I too was reminded of how innocent and naive I was at this age. It was obvious to see from my journaling that the most important things to me at this time of my life were my friendships and grades. The furthest thing from my mind was anything to do with sex or stimulation. In fact, I'm not even sure I knew what either were at this age. But even if I did, it is so important that I recognize I had zero control over this person and I was a victim of a terrible crime, and so were you.

Then I began to wonder, why did the abuse happen to me? I learned most often years of pornography, planning, and fantasizing about sexually abusing someone is the history of an abuser. It is my firm belief, after a lot of study about sexual abuse, that if I had not been accessible to my abuser, with no fault of my own, they would have abused someone else or they would have waited for a better opportunity. In fact, most abusers do abuse more than just one child. It has nothing to do with the child, but in making the fantasies they have created in their head become reality. Yuck!

9 Sutherland, 35.

Let's look into this even further. The National Association of Adult Survivors of Child Abuse reveals that, "*ap-proximately forty-two million adult survivors of child-hood sexual abuse live in America today.*"[10]

That is ONLY in America, and the cases that are RE-PORTED!! Did you know that sexual abuse is severely underreported? Why? Many of the reasons include embarrassment, fear of being blamed, fear of not being believed or misunderstood, fear of being harmed or causing harm to others, and the list goes on and on. Maybe one of those cases is you, and can you blame yourself or others who do not report it?

Now I want you to ask yourself, is it possible for that many children just in America alone, to have done something or had the power to cause an adult to sexually abuse them? Not a chance. We are not that powerful over others even as an adult, let alone a young child or teenager. Therefore, for many reasons, the truth is, the abuse simply could not have been and was not my fault or your fault. We must accept this in order to move forward on our roads to recovery.

10 Sutherland, 32.

I love this statement by Crystal M Sutherland, author of Journey to Heal, and could not agree more. *"We may not always like the truth, but the truth will always set us free from the lies we've believed."* [11]

Lies? Help me understand more. Am I living lies? Well, I was living a lie for a few years that the abuse was my fault, are you living this or other lies connected to your abuse? Once you are able to identify these lies, you can begin to work on freeing yourself from the guilt and shame you have been carrying as you have blamed yourself. This takes me to our next step of overcoming. Truths and Lies.

Let's help you identify some lies you may have been living and understand how to free yourself of those un-truths.

When I first met Kimberly Watts, life coach of 15 plus years, she saw deep pain in me. She could tell by my actions and demeanor that I was trying to hide and deal with something very painful. She cared for me, spent time with me asking questions and introduced me to something called 'Truths and Lies'.

11 Sutherland, *Journey to Heal.*

To help you understand this concept, let me ask you a few questions. Have you ever tried to overcome some-thing? Anything? Weight Loss, anger, alcoholism, drug abuse, stealing, etc. How did that work out for you? Was it hard? Harder than you anticipated? Yea, me too.

In the book Atomic Habits, by James Clear, he intro-duces the three levels of behavioral change: Identity/be-lief, process/actions, and desired outcome. He teaches that in order for a person to reach true behavioral change they must pass through each of these stages starting from the inside out.[12]

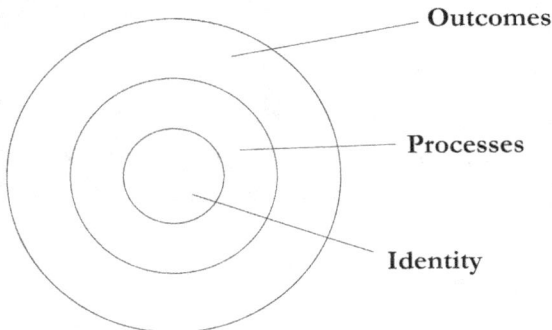

Image of 3 levels of behavioral change by James Clear.

12 Clear, *Atomic Habits*, 22.

Most people who desire change naturally start from the outside and work inward. For example, if you wanted to lose weight what would that look like for you? I would decide I needed to lose a few pounds after looking in the mirror and thinking "I'm too fat" or "I need to lose weight." Next, I would figure out how much weight I wanted to lose and come up with an exercising and eating plan to help me reach my goal. Does that sound familiar?

Would it surprise you if I told you that is exactly why most of us fail and never reach our desired outcome? Or that is why we are unable to keep the weight off? We try making a behavioral change by working from the outside in. We only have so much willpower before we give up and decide it was a waste of time anyway. So how do we make true behavioral change?

My wise friend Mrs. Kimberly Watts added a fourth level: Truths. This level goes right in the middle and is where we must start if we want true behavioral change.

13 Clear, *Atomic Habits*.

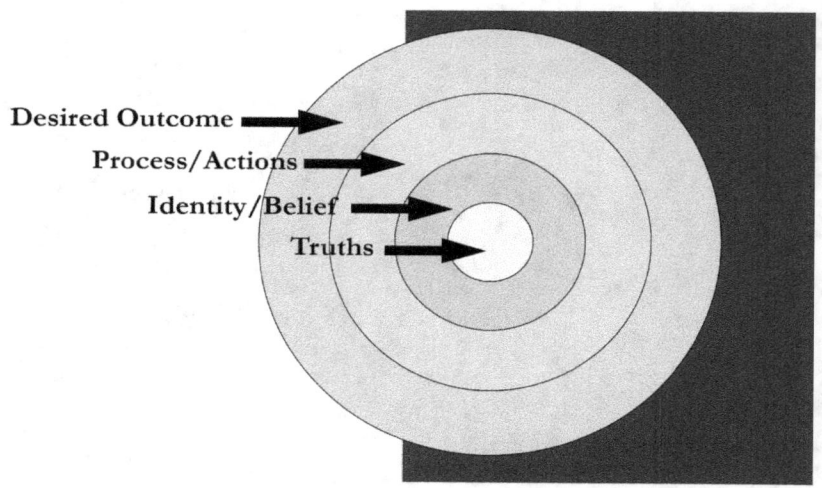

Image of 4 levels of behavioral change by Kimberly Watts.[14]
Let's walk you through how to achieve true behavioral change.

How to Identify the Truths

First, ask yourself, why do I want to lose weight? The answers will most likely be a more superficial layer of what you think are truths, but are in actuality the lies.

1. When I look in the mirror, I look disgusting.

2. I hate the way I feel.

3. When others look at me, they think I have a problem.

4. I'm too fat to influence others.

5. Etc.

14 Kimberly Watts, "True Behavioral Change (Graph)," 2021.

Then ask yourself, what is holding me back from losing weight and keeping it off?

You may write:

1. I have a Thyroid problem.

2. I have an emotional addiction to food (eating comforts me).

3. I can't control myself around food.

4. Food is my enemy.

5. Etc.

Now look at both lists and pick out those statements that may be truly how you feel, but are actually lies you have been telling yourself. For example, *I'm too fat to influence others*. While you may really feel this way, this is a lie. Many overweight individuals are very influential.

Second example, *when I look in the mirror, I look dis-gusting*. Again, this may really be how you feel, but you are not disgusting. This is a lie you have heard some-where that has caused you to repeat over and over that overweight individuals are disgusting, leading you to believe that you are disgusting as well. The truth is, you are beautiful, and you have purpose just the way you are.

Third example, *when others look at me, they think I have a problem*. Again, you may truly feel this way, but it is not the truth. It is something you have been wired to believe from something you have heard somewhere along your way. The truth is, it doesn't matter what other people think. You can't control that, but you can control how you truly feel about yourself. You are amazing. You can overcome whatever you want to, and you have infinite worth.

Did you identify the lies on the list above? Now let me teach you how to turn them into truths. Start by crossing off the lie and writing the exact opposite, or what you wish you were. For example,

Lie: When I look in the mirror, I look disgusting.

Truth: I am beautiful just the way I am.

Lie: I'm too fat to influence others.

Truth: I can influence many people for good. It is completely up to me and has nothing to do with my weight. I have purpose.

Lie: I hate the way I feel.

Truth: I love my body. It serves me every day by allowing me to do many things.

Lie: When others look at me, they think I have a problem.

Truth: I am amazing. I can overcome anything I really want to. I have infinite worth.

Lie: Food is my enemy.

Truth: Food is my fuel. When I eat nutritious food, it makes me feel good. When I eat unhealthy options, my body doesn't like it.

Now let's draw our attention to the other three. *I have a thyroid problem. I have an emotional addiction to food. I can't control myself around food.* These three we need to look at a little deeper. Each one needs to be addressed to have true behavioral change. If you have a thyroid problem, telling yourself you don't is not going to change the fact that your thyroid is releasing too much or not enough hormone. If you have an emotional addiction to food, you need to figure out why and begin dealing with that issue to truly see behavioral change. The same is true about *I can't control myself around food.* Why? Figure out the root cause and ask for professional advice to help you overcome.

As you are working on the last three you don't have to wait to start your change. Take the list of truths above and add any additional ones you would like to believe about yourself when it comes to the weight.

Truths:

- I am beautiful just the way I am.
- I can influence many people for good. It is completely up to me. I have purpose.
- I love my body. It serves me every day by al-lowing me to do many things.
- I am amazing. I can overcome anything I really want to. I have infinite worth.
- Food is my fuel. When I eat nutritious food, it makes me feel good. When I eat unhealthy options, my body doesn't feel well.
- I can take responsibility for my weight.

Now each day start repeating these truths to yourself out loud at least every morning and night. Trust me on this, I know how you are feeling. I have been there. It was very uncomfortable to repeat these things to myself in the beginning because I had believed the opposite for so long. But they are truths and just like it took time for you to believe those lies, it is going to take time for you to change your way of thinking and truly begin to believe these truths. You will be amazed at how fast you start to feel the change taking place, if you will take this exercise seriously and do the daily work.

Once you start believing the truths and begin working on overcoming the others that may take extra time and help, you will naturally find yourself in the next layer of identity/belief. You are forming and believing a new true identity as you do this work. Don't quit, this work needs to be done daily even as you move into the next layer.

Process and Actions

It is now time to figure out the daily steps you will need to take to lose the weight, such as exercise and a nutrition plan. Once again, as you do this, do not forget to include the new actions of repeating the truths and working on the other issues needing to be resolved. It will be a process, but so worth it because this is creating true behavioral change. Repeating these actions over and over along with the process and actions daily will lead to your desired outcome and long-term behavioral change. Does that make sense?

Now let's look at an example from my story and the abuse. I didn't know about the three levels of behavioral change at that time, but as I examined my story of over-coming, I could clearly see that I had worked through each of these steps with my counselor. It made perfect sense why I was able to have positive, true behavioral change all those years ago.

Example #1:

The first thing I did was identify the behavior I wanted to change. That was easy, the depression and anxiety were ruining my life. I then asked myself, *What thoughts am I repeating that could be causing the con-stant sadness and bouts of* anxiety? I identified feelings of inner turmoil every single time I wondered if the abuse was my fault. I felt shame and guilt as I rehearsed the things others had said and I worried they may be true. I distanced and withdrew myself from others and wanted to sleep every chance I got. I was short-tempered and extremely unhappy with myself and cried constantly.

Lie #1: The abuse was my fault.

As I look back, I can clearly see the change that took place in my attitude and zeal for life once I understood and then believed that the abuse not only was not my fault, but there was nothing I could have done to antagonize or stop the abuse from happening. It had nothing to do with ME. Therapy helped me to understand this as a young girl and at a vital period of my life.

Truth #1: The abuse was in no way, shape, or form my fault.

Because I then truly believed it was not my fault, I had unknowingly mastered the *truths* and the *identity and beliefs* levels. My actions naturally changed from with-drawing myself and desiring to sleep all day long, to craving the company of my friends as many hours a day as possible.

Many times, once the **true belief** is there, the actions come naturally without even thinking about what you need to do to overcome the behavior. This was my experience. The actions came naturally and before long I had reached my desired outcome of ridding my life of the debilitating depression and anxiety. It is important to note, the depression never fully went away, and I still deal with it on a minimal level today, but I now know how to rid myself of the overwhelming depression and the crippling anxiety. Sometimes I feel no symptoms at all, and other times I am consciously fighting it by repeating truths. And it works!!

Example #2:

The second behavior I was determined to overcome was the constant, intense anger. I asked myself, *What is causing the anger?* At that time, soon after the abuse, I had convinced myself, from my own thoughts and feelings as well as the opinions I heard from others, that sexual abuse of a child was an unforgivable act. I could not fathom how anyone could ever get to the point of doing something like this to a child or anyone else. I did not understand it and it angered me to the core. My days were spent billowing in the hatred and scheming how I could get back at Bob. I wanted him to feel what I had felt and hurt like I was hurting. I wanted his life to feel ruined and over and I was sure if I thought long and hard enough about it, I could come up with a way. These thoughts and feelings consumed every minute of every day for a couple of years. It was a very dark and miserable time of my life.

Lie #2: Sexual abuse of a child is an unforgivable act.

One day, I remember hearing a comment that took me back. *"Holding a grudge and deciding not to forgive someone damages the victim much more than it ever punishes the perpetrator (unknown)."* What? That doesn't make sense. Well, at least it didn't at that moment. Did I have it all backwards? How would unforgiveness hurt me and not Bob? As I talked to my counselor, she explained the detrimental effects our thoughts can have on us when they are negative. And many times, our anger doesn't even affect our perpetrator be-cause they are completely unaware of our thinking. The more we focus on hurting others, the more we will hurt ourselves. She went on to share that forgiveness does not mean I was approving what had happened to me, but I was choosing to let it go in order to free *myself* of the grudge, anger and pain.

My conclusion: *The anger and hatred were ruining me, and not affecting my abuser at all. If I wanted to heal and be set free, I had to stop focusing on him and start focusing on me. Just because I was choosing to forgive didn't mean I was freeing Bob or letting him get away with what had happened. I needed to allow my higher power to worry about Bob's fate, not me. It was much more important for me to focus on MY happiness.*

Truth #2: Forgiveness does not mean approval of the act. Forgiveness sets *ME* free.

Then came the *process and actions*. Even after I knew what my counselor was telling me was true, it still took time for me to truly process this new truth and believe it. The actions were even harder but became easier and easier as I made the concerted effort to apply them. The anger didn't go away immediately, and each time it would start I would have to consciously remind myself that letting it go was for my advantage and I wanted to feel happy again so badly that I continued reminding myself of this new truth. I wish I had known then, that repeating the new truth to myself many times a day would help me get the results even quicker. But some-how, I made it. I remember feeling changes happen quite quickly after acknowledging and believing this new truth, and a few months later, I felt so much lighter, I was feeling happiness again, the damaging feelings no longer consumed me, and I was liberated.

Here's a reminder of the 4 steps to behavioral change: Truths, Identity/Belief, Process/Actions, and Desired Outcome.

Step by Step Instructions to achieve true behavioral change:

1. Identify the behavior you want to change

2. Identify the lie you are living that is causing this behavior. Ask yourself why am I depressed and anxious? What am I worrying about?
3. Turn that lie into a truth.

4. Repeat that truth over and over until you begin to believe it.

5. Process the new truth and take actions each day that solidify that new truth.

6. Desired outcome will be achieved.

Ok, now it's your turn! Are you ready? Just follow the steps above one by one and if you get stuck go back and read my examples to help you through. This is going to take a lot of honesty with yourself. Many times, we are in denial of some of the negativities in our life and sometimes it just feels like it is going to be too hard to change them. Let me remind you, nothing good comes without work.

First, make a list of behaviors in your life you would like to change. For example: anger, self-hate, self-harm, sub-stance abuse, rage, compulsive spending, comfort eating or starving yourself, negativity, irritability, physically/emotionally abusing someone else, etc. Now, take your list and ask yourself what are your deepest thoughts when you are involved in this behavior? What are you trying to cover up or deal with? Examples: *I am worth-less, No one will ever want me, I should have prevented the abuse, I wish I wouldn't have…, I wish I could cause my abuser pain, I hate my abuser for ruining my life, Why, did God let this happen to me? Etc.*

Now let's take each of those possible thoughts and state the lie you are living if you are telling yourself any of these.

Thought: *I am worthless.*

Lie: The abuse has ruined me. I'm not deserving of anything good.

Thought: *No one will ever want me.*

Lie: The abuse has ruined me. I'm not deserving of a good person in my life.

Thought: *I should have prevented the abuse.*

Lie: The abuse was my fault.

Thought: *I wish I wouldn't have….*

Lie: The abuse was my fault.

Thought: *I wish I could cause my abuser pain.*

Lie: It is my job to make sure my abuser pays for the abuse.

Thought: *I hate my abuser for ruining my life.*

Lie: My life is ruined because of the abuse.

Thought: *Why did God let this happen to me?*

Lie: God does not love me. God is punishing me for…

Thought: *I cannot believe someone could do some-thing so disgusting.*

Lie: I will never forgive my abuser.

Remember, a lot of times the lies are hard to identify because you have believed them for so long. So let me help you with identifying lies. What do you tell yourself that causes you to shrink, feel inadequate, holds you back, or keeps you from becoming your best self or be-ing happy? Those are most likely your lies! If it is easier for you to identify your lies this way that is totally fine. Write down the lie and then ask yourself what kind of behaviors do you participate in to try and cover up these lies or feelings of failure or inadequacy?

For example: *What do I tell myself that causes me to shrink or feel inadequate in life? I am a terrible mother.* Your lie is: I am a terrible mother. I will never be able to be what my children need. Then ask yourself what do I do to cover up the fact that I feel like a terrible mother? I distance myself from my children, I feel over-whelmed with all I have to do to be considered a good mom. I want to sleep all the time to cover up the pain. Behavior I want to change: Depression and feelings of being overwhelmed and like I am not enough.

Does that make sense?

Now what do we do with these new lies we have found? Write a list, then one at a time cross them off and write the opposite or what you wish you were.

Even if you do not believe the opposite at all! Write it!! This is your new truth.

Example:

Lie: I'm not deserving of anything good.
Truth: Whomever I marry will be so lucky. I can be-come anything
     I want to become.
Lie: The abuse was my fault.
Truth: The abuse had nothing to do with me, and it was absolutely
     not my fault.

Lie: It is my job to make sure my abuser pays for the abuse.

Truth: It is not my job to punish my abuser, I will focus on my happiness alone.

Lie: My life is ruined because of the abuse.

Truth: I am powerful, the abuse will make me a better and stronger person.

Lie: God does not love me. God is punishing me for... Truth: God loves me so much that He has allowed an opportunity for me to become more like Him. God will help me every step of the way if I want Him to.

Lie: I will never forgive my abuser. Sexual abuse in un-forgivable.

Truth: Forgiveness is for my happiness alone and does not mean I am ok with what happened.

Was that hard? Again, it is totally normal to not believe the new truths you have written. Remember, it took time for you to believe the lies you have been living, it is going to take time to reverse those lies as well. Just trust me on this one.

Now write a list of all of your new truths only!! Keep this list next to your bed or posted on your fridge or bathroom mirror and repeat these new truths to yourself out loud every morning and every night at least. Soon you will have them memorized and I encourage you to recite them over and over in your mind throughout the day. It will be difficult at first, especially because you probably won't believe them, but I promise you change is happening and pretty soon it will bring a smile to your face as you recite, and a desire to become those new truths will begin. Pay close attention to your new actions, desires and feelings as you start believing these new truths.

What's next? *Process and Actions*

As you begin processing and believing these new truths, you may notice you start to do things you didn't do before. For example, if one of the truths you are reciting is *I can become anything I want to become,* you may find as you continue reciting this daily, your mind may make a shift and you may naturally start feeling lighter, happier, more excited for the future, etc. Continue acting on these new feelings and enjoy every minute of it. This is a new truth you are speaking to yourself.

Also, take the time to come up with some actions you can commit to each day that will help you become whatever it is that you want to become. For example, if you want to become an author, begin down the path of writing your first book. Start brainstorming ideas or researching and asking around to those who can guide you on making this a reality.

If you want to become the best mother in the world, then ask yourself, *what would that look like for me?* Maybe you came up with: I would listen intently to my children when they talk to me. I will not raise my voice. I will spend 15 minutes a day of uninterrupted time with each child. Now it's time to act on these identified actions. Get excited! True behavioral change will come as you truly believe and take action steps towards these new truths.

Remember, change will not happen overnight, but it is very possible for you to notice change starting very quickly, like even day 2 or three. Give it time and don't give up! These are the steps to true behavioral change.

Side note: Go back to the list you made when you asked yourself, *what is holding me back from accomplishing*

_____ *(a certain behavioral change)?* If there are any you can identify as not being able to overcome with speaking truth and taking action, you may need some extra help to overcome. For example, when you asked yourself, *what is keeping me from losing weight and keeping it off?* If you listed: I have a thyroid problem or I have an emotional connection with food, receiving help from a professional will help you get these under control so you can be more successful with your goal.

CHAPTER 4

RELATIONSHIP WITH GOD/HIGHER POWER

Creating a relationship with God was paramount to my recovery and healing. If you are not a religious person or you do not believe in a higher power, that is completely fine. But hang with me for just a minute. If you are entirely uncomfortable with this topic, then skip to the next chapter, but I encourage you to just stop for one moment, open your heart, and hear my story.

All growing up my family was religious and we were active members of The Church of Jesus Christ of Latter-Day Saints. I had always believed in God and His son Jesus Christ, or at least hoped what I had been taught about them up to this point in my life was true. After the turmoil and confusion set in from the abuse, I was desperate to know for sure if they were real.

Who is God and Who am I?

I had been taught since I could remember that God was an all-powerful being who had created me in His image, created everything in the world I was living, and sacrificed His son for me and all of His children. Jesus agreed to sacrifice His life and perform the atonement so that I could be forgiven of my sins and live with Him, my Heavenly Father (God) and my family eternally after I die.

I had also been taught that I was a daughter of God, He knew me personally, knew of my struggles, loved me more than I could ever comprehend, and His son knew exactly how to help me through anything because He had experienced everything in the act of dying for me. But did he love ME? Did he really know ME? I had to know for myself.

I began reading the Book of Mormon (a book of scripture in my religion) every single night before bed desperate for some kind of answer. Shortly after I began, I read 1st Nephi 3:7, it reads: *"And it came to pass that I, Nephi, said unto my father: I will go and do the things which the Lord hath commanded, for I know that the Lord giveth no commandments unto the children of men, save he shall prepare a way for them that they may accomplish the thing which he commandeth them."* [15]

That verse jumped off the page at me and I was filled with warmth and peace from my head to my toes, something I had never experienced before. I felt that had to be God speaking to me and expressing that He knew my situation, He knew and understood my pain, and was telling me if I would let Him help me, I could and would make it through this difficult time. I recognized God had heard me, He had answered me, and it was now up to me to allow Him to show me the way through.

I began pleading to my Heavenly Father daily for strength to first overcome the anger and resentment, and I slowly saw miracles start to unfold in my own life. Each experience solidified what I was hoping was true and it felt so good to have someone all powerful and all-knowing on my side. He did know what I was feeling, just as I had been taught in Alma 7:12, *"And he will take upon him death, that he may lose the bands of death which bind his people; and he will take upon him their infirmities, that his bowels may be filled with mercy, according to the flesh, that he may know ac-cording to the flesh how to succor his people according to their infirmities."* [16]

15   Smith, *The Book of Mormon.*

I can tell you with all the energy of my soul, that these daily prayers, reading of my scriptures and trusting in the Lord are some of the core reasons I was able to continue through the healing process over the next few very painful years and come out victorious.

Over time, my prayers changed from pleading and beg-ging Him to fix the situation and take it all away, to accepting the abuse and asking for strength to keep on pushing through something that I could now see He completely understood. As time passed, my relationship with my Heavenly Father was strengthened, I leaned on Him for everything and often felt His presence. It was not easy, but so much easier than it had felt before. If given the opportunity, I would never want to go back and try to do it all over again on my own. No way! Not now that I knew how much easier it was with Him.

A friend gave me the poem Footprints in The Sand by Carolyn Joyce Carty, not long after the abuse and I felt that it explained what was happening in my life perfectly.

16   Smith.

One night a man had a dream. He dreamed he was walking
along the beach with the LORD. Across the sky flashed scenes
from his life. For each scene he noticed two sets of footprints in the
sand:
one belonging to him, the other to the LORD.

When the last scene of his life flashed before him,
he looked back at the footprints in the sand.
He noticed that many times along the path of
his life there was only one set of footprints.

He also noticed that it happened at the very lowest and saddest times of his life. This really bothered him and he questioned the LORD about it: "LORD, you said that once I decided to follow you, you'd walk with me all the way.

But I have noticed that during the most troublesome times in my life, there is only one set of footprints. I don't understand why when I needed you most you would leave me."

The LORD replied: "My son, my precious child, I love you and I would never leave you. During your times of trial and suffering, when you see only one set of footprints, it was then that I carried you." [17]

As I reached different milestones in my journey of healing, my faith and trust in the Lord grew stronger and stronger and I soon depended on Him being there and believed fully that He would be. And He was. He didn't ever take it all away, as I had hoped and knew He could, but He never left my side.

17   Carty, "Footprints in the Sand," 77.

God has promised in Mathew 11:28, 29, *"Come unto me, all ye that are heavy laden, and I will give you rest. Take my yoke upon you, and learn of me; for I am meek and lowly in heart: and ye shall find rest unto your souls."*[18] Because I took the time to seek Him out and ask for His help, He opened the door and did as He had promised.

As I have faced further challenges, I learned to always turn to Him first for guidance, strength and direction. He has made lemonade out of lemons many times in my life throughout the years, so much so that in the last couple of years I have decided it is time I fully turn my life over to Him and allow Him to be in charge. Each time I have done this, He has turned a hardship into something more beautiful in my life than I could have ever created on my own.

Music became a way for me to hear Him answering my prayers. A year or so ago I was introduced to the song *You Say* by Lauren Daigle and it quickly became the song I played over and over when my feelings of inadequacy would begin to creep back in. It was the answer I was looking for.

18   Mat. 11: 28-29 (Authorized King James Version).

"I keep fighting voices in my mind that say I'm not enough. Every single lie that tells me I will never measure up. Am I more than just the sum of every high and every low? Remind me once again just who I am because I need to know.

You say I am loved, when I can't feel a thing.
You say I am strong, when I think I am weak.
You say I am held, when I am falling short.
When I don't belong, oh you say I am yours.

And I believe, oh I believe, what you say to me.
I believe. Oh, I believe. What you say to me. I believe.
The only thing that matters now is everything you think of me.
In you I find my worth, in you I find my identity.

You say I am loved, when I can't feel a thing.
You say I am strong, when I think I am weak.
You say I am held, when I am falling short.
When I don't belong, oh you say I am yours.

And I believe, oh I believe, what you say to me.
I believe. Oh, I believe. What you say to me.
I believe. Taking all I have and now I'm laying it at your feet.
You have every failure God; you have every victory.

You say I am loved, when I can't feel a thing. You say I am strong, when I think I am weak. You say I am held, when I am falling short. When I don't belong, oh you say I am yours. And I believe, oh I believe, what you say to me. I believe. Oh, I believe. Yes, I believe, what you say to me. I believe."[19]

I have truly come to know that life is going to continue throwing hard things my way. I'm going to continue having times of feeling like I am not enough, but it is up to me to invite Him in to remind me that I am His, He loves me and all that really matters is what He thinks of me. I also know the Lord is on my side and He will never leave me. When I am troubled by something out of my control, I have the option of laying everything at His feet and allowing Him to take care of the problem. What a weight this knowledge has lifted.

Why does God allow hard things to happen to us?

I now know and believe that God loves us unconditionally (yes that means you too) and *"no one is immune from the challenges of life, nor does personal righteousness remove us from, or personal wickedness cause us to experience difficulties that will stretch our character. Trials are an integral part of our experience here on earth"*[20] and are for OUR good. Did you catch that? Have you ever wondered if the abuse was a punishment to you from God for doing something wrong? Well, if you have the answer is no! Trials do not come as punishments, but *"the very opportunity for us to face adversity and affliction is evidence of our Heavenly Father's and Savior's infinite love,"*[21] explains President Eyring.

19. Daigle, *You Say (Official Music Video)*

How are hardships evidence of God's love? I believe God wants nothing more than to bring each one of us back into His presence after we die. But, in order for us to live with God again, we have to be prepared to embrace His glorious presence. Trials humble us and oftentimes give us opportunities to develop intimate rela-tionships with God and come to know His true character. This dependence and increased faith in Him help to prepare us for that day.

Trials are for OUR good? How so? Jesus taught, *"And if thou shouldst be cast into the pit, or into the hands of murderers, and the sentence of death passed upon thee; if thou be cast into the deep; if the billowing surge con-spire against thee; if fierce winds become thine enemy; if the heavens gather blackness, and all the elements combine to hedge up the way; and above all, if the very jaws of hell shall gape open the mouth wide after thee, know thou, my son, that all these things shall give thee experience, and shall be for thy good."* [22]

20 "Asheville Ward News."
21 Eyring, "Adversity."Henry B. Eyring taught,

"The greatest blessing that will come when we prove ourselves faithful to our covenants during our trials will be a change in our natures. By our choosing to keep our covenants, the power of Jesus Christ and the blessings of His Atonement can work in us. Our hearts can be softened to love, to for-give, and to invite others to come unto the Savior. Our confidence in the Lord increases. Our fears decrease." [23]

I recently learned that there are three reasons hard/bad things happen to us.

1. Our own poor choices
2. Poor choices of others
3. God's way of preparing us to become like Him (polishing us into the best version of ourselves).

22 Smith and Cowdery, *The Doctrine and Covenants of the Churchof Jesus Christ of Latter Day Saints.*
23 Eyring, "Tested, Proved, and Polished."

I also believe God allows tough things to happen to us so that we can learn to trust and lean on Him and eventually become more like Him. Many times, I have wished He would stop some things from happening, but that too is part of His plan. He gave each of His children their own agency in order to learn and grow and He can't take that agency away from us. But He is just waiting for us to invite Him in to guide and strengthen us along the way, no matter the hardship. I further believe difficult circumstances can do one of two things to or for us. They can harden our hearts and lead to self-destructive behaviors, or they can soften our hearts and help us to see His individual plan of happiness for each one of us. I also believe there is no better way to learn compassion and see others the way God does, than to struggle through something unbearable ourselves, learn to rely on Him and feel His strength and love for us, and come out victorious. Remember, He also taught, *"Ye cannot behold with your natural eyes, for the pre-sent time, the design of your God concerning those things which shall come hereafter, and the glory which shall follow after much tribulation. For after much tribulation come the blessings."*[24]

Sometimes the hardest thing to do in the midst of a trial is to wait for time to heal all wounds. Although I have found this to be true, I have also learned in the mean-time, as I chose to include God in the process of over-coming, I can rely on those blessings to come.

The greatest blessings I have received and recognized after pushing through a trial is my own transformation into someone stronger and more Christlike. Somehow this transformation makes all of the pain and anguish worth it. I know this can happen for you too.

24 Smith and Cowdery,
The Doctrine and Covenants of the Church of Jesus Christ of Latter Day Saints.

What is my purpose?

As we grow and develop into beings much like our Sav-ior, we are then able to see others through His eyes and assist them through their challenges as well. He needs our hands to guide and direct others with our experiences and growth. There were specific people along my path who were able to guide me through with their love, compassion, and experience and I am forever grateful for them. I hope I can now be a hand that can do the same for you.

What were the benefits of inviting my higher power into my journey to healing?

- Feeling loved and understood
- Knowing someone else was always by my side who understood exactly what I was going through
- Daily strength beyond my own to push through
- Understanding my purpose
- Understanding why God was not taking it all away

Where do I begin if I might want to see if God/Higher Power can help me too?

Truly have a desire to know.
- Simply ask in your mind or out loud if He/She/Higher Power knows YOU and loves YOU personally.
- Sit in stillness and pay close attention to how you feel.
- Do not give up if you feel nothing for a while.
- Persistence is key. I believe God is seeing if you really want to know He is real. Be patient with Him as He is with you.
- Tell Him you need Him and want Him to be a part of your life every single day.

- Make time for stillness each day to read scripture, listen to spiritual music, or to just meditate. God does not speak in a loud voice. It will be in times of stillness that you will hear or feel Him.
- When you feel something, thank Him for answering you.
- Take time for Him each day, talk to Him as if He is sitting right beside you. Pour your heart out to Him. Tell Him your worries and concerns and ask for His guidance. Then listen…
- Do what He tells you. If it is something good, you can trust it is from Him. Follow through and He will continue to give you more as you demonstrate your willingness to hear and trust Him.

About a year ago I came across a song David Archuleta sings based on the scripture that answered my prayers and gave me strength to move on so many years ago. The scripture again is 3 Nephi 3:7: *"And it came to pass that I, Nephi, said unto my father: I will go and do the things which the Lord hath commanded, for I know that the Lord giveth no commandments unto the children of men, save he shall prepare a way for them that they may accomplish the thing which he commandeth them."*25

The song is called *I will Go and Do*. I wish I had had this song then to constantly remind me of the answer I had received from my Savior, so I am giving it to you now in hopes that it will be a reminder that you are never alone, unless you choose to be (many people push Him away). God's strength, direction and love are waiting to assist you along your path to healing and recovery, He's just waiting for you to ask for it. I know He loves you unconditionally and will ease your burdens and provide a way for you to overcome as well.

25   Smith, *The Book of Mormon.*

"No matter where I go, I know I'm not alone. I feel my Savior there beside me. He leads me through the night, He's always been my guide. He promised He will never leave me. Though my burdens seem too much to bear, He'll bless me. So, whatever He commands,

I will go and do. I will stand for truth. Though the world may back away, I will walk right through. I know if I follow Him, follow Him in Faith. He will ease my burdens, and He'll provide a way. He'll provide a way.

When I feel overcome and all my strength is gone, I think of all the ways He's blessed me. My journey may seem long, but He'll lift me with His love. A perfect love that's never ending. He will give me, give me all the strength I needed. So, whatever He commands,

I will go and do. I will stand for truth. Though the world may back away, I will walk right through. I know if I follow Him, follow Him in Faith. He will ease my burdens, and He'll provide a way. He'll provide a way for me to cross the desert, to set across the ocean.

If that's where He sends me, I'll follow His plan. I'll do whatever He commands me for I know that He will lead me to the promised land. I will go and do. I will stand for truth. Though the world may shut Him out, I will make Him room. I know if I follow Him, follow Him in Faith.

He will ease my burdens and He'll provide a way.
He'll provide a way. He'll provide a way.26
No matter where I go, I know I'm not alone,

I feel my Savior there beside me."

The relationship I have developed with my Heavenly Father is the most precious gift I have been given. It took work, as all good things do. But now knowing the difference between facing something alone or with God, I know I can face anything without question as long as I have Him by my side.

I pray that you can develop your own personal relation-ship and come to understand exactly what I have experienced for yourself.

26   Archuleta, *I Will Go and Do.*

CHAPTER 5

FORGIVENESS

I get it, I get it, forgiveness is another one of those subjects that are oftentimes at the very bottom of the to-do list for a victim of sexual abuse, if even on the list at all. Again, I ask that you hang with me for a moment and do your best to open your heart and hear my story.

For years after my abuse, the thought of forgiveness made my heart pound and my stomach feel like hurling. I had convinced myself that what had happened to me was not only unforgivable, but one of the sickest acts a human could ever do to another. No way was I ever going to let my abuser off the hook to enjoy his life again. I would hate him and hurt him until the day I died. I was determined to make him suffer the way he had caused me suffering. Can any of you relate?

I just want you to think for a couple of seconds how you felt as you read those last few sentences. My explanation would be darkness and misery. If I had really continued living the rest of my life day in and day out with the objective to cause my abuser pain, can you imagine how much energy and valuable time that would have taken, not to mention the detrimental effects it would have had on my future life and family?

Thankfully, a few years after the abuse, my heart began to soften as I cultivated a relationship with God. As I grew, I made silly decisions and hurt others unintentionally. Sometimes to the point I was completely ashamed and begged for their forgiveness. I started to recognize that I too needed forgiveness from others. It was at this time that I realized the need for me to forgive my abuser as well. If I wanted and expected others to have compassion towards me and let go of the mistakes I made, I too needed to consider this for those who had hurt me. But sexual abuse, rape, murder, etc. were much worse than other simple mistakes. I would catch myself wanting to justify in an attempt to change my own mind. But were they? Are wrongdoings placed on a list of severity? How do we decide which are forgivable and which aren't? Are there in fact some acts that we do not need to forgive?

It was at this time I heard of a story that changed my heart forever. A family was traveling home on a Friday evening after having a night out together. They were broadsided by a drunk teenager. The pregnant wife, one son and a daughter were instantly killed. The father and younger son somehow survived. Within days of the accident, the father made a statement I would never for-get. He met with the drunk driver and calmly told him that he had forgiven him and that he should forgive himself as well. The father said soon after the accident he had an overwhelming feeling that he needed to let it go. When he spoke with the young man, he also told him to pick a date and then make a decision to move on and forget about what had happened from that date forward. He said it was incredibly difficult to learn les-sons of love this way, but it was so worth letting that burden go. After the forgiveness, he felt he could continue on with his new life.

This blew my mind. How could he be so forgiving and do it so quickly? His life was shattered. He had admitted his life had been devastated in an instant, but he still chose to forgive. The peace and calm I felt from that man was moving. How was he able to do this?

I tried putting myself in his shoes and concluded I didn't think I would ever be able to forgive someone who had chosen to drink, drive and in turn had killed my spouse, parents, or anyone close to me. That was an unforgivable act. Or was it? Once again two different perspectives.

A few months later I was made aware of another situation. I heard about a dentist in my little community who had become addicted to narcotics. Because of the ad-diction, he was doing everything possible to get the meds he needed on a daily basis. Even if that meant be-traying patients, illegal prescription writing, and lying to everyone around him. He eventually lost his practice and was sent to jail. His wife, completely unaware of what was going on, had a decision to make. Should I hate him and divorce him, or should I forgive and sup-port him through his trial?

Can you imagine the betrayal, anger, and resentment she must have felt? I'm sure many would agree this is an unforgivable act. She decided to stand by his side as he fought through recovery. They faced humiliating comments from the community on top of all of the hurt they were already feeling from the addiction and loss of his practice. This went on for years.

You should see them today! He has become a new per-son through this trial. He is now sharing his experience and how he was able to overcome it on social media to help others in need. He did all that was needed to get his license back and is currently practicing dentistry again today. When you hear him speak, you can feel his light. When I think of this situation, I can't help but think what if his cute wife would have decided not to forgive? So much goodness has come from this mistake and forgiveness.

I had to admit to myself that I would rather be in my situation than either of the ones I had heard about. For once, I felt like I got the better end of the deal even in my terrible situation. That's when I decided, if they could forgive such tremendous acts, then why couldn't I?

The lesson I learned was none of us are exempt from hurting others intentionally or unintentionally in life. Some may seem more serious than others, depending on the viewpoint of the individual. Some are more visible to the public eye, and others are hidden in silence. But all acts cause some sort of pain and anger no matter how big or small. What it really boils down to is, when we choose not to forgive others, no matter the act, we become resentful and bitter. Both are like drinking poi-son and can eventually destroy our lives physically, mentally and emotionally. Forgiveness is paramount for our own happiness and survival and has nothing to do with the severity of the act done against us.

Are there other reasons to forgive?

During my times of severe bitterness, when I couldn't even stand the thought of liberating my abuser, I read something that opened my eyes. When you forgive someone, you are not forgetting or excusing what they did but more importantly, you are releasing yourself of the burden and control that unforgiveness places on your soul. Forgiveness brings the kind of peace that helps you move on with your life. *Wait a minute? Once again, forgiveness is for me?* That was an ah-ha moment!! At this very time, I was really struggling and began searching for any possible way to relieve myself of the burden I was carrying. I was open to this new ad-vice.

The thoughts continued, *but was holding a grudge a burden to me?* I had figured promising myself to never forgive was all about hurting my abuser, not myself. As I reviewed the past few months and all the time and energy, I had spent thinking about how I could get re-venge and cause my abuser anguish, I realized it was definitely affecting my life in a negative way, and was not punishing my abuser one bit. He had no idea what I was stewing about inside, I hadn't told him, so how did I figure my actions would punish him at all. It was only negatively affecting me. I decided I was no longer going to let *his* decisions destroy *my life*. I needed to forgive, for *me*.

What are the benefits of forgiveness?

FREEDOM!! Yes, I will say it again, FREEDOM! The day I realized I was no longer in charge of causing my abuser pain (I would leave that to someone else), I felt free! Like an elephant had been removed from my shoulders. I suddenly had an entire new list of things to think about, and I began focusing on myself, my happiness, and becoming the best me.

The Mayo Clinic teaches, "letting go of grudges and bitterness can make way for improved health and peace of mind. Forgiveness can lead to:

- Healthier relationships
- Improved mental health
- Less anxiety, stress and hostility
- Lower blood pressure
- Fewer symptoms of depression
- A stronger immune system
- Improved heart health
- Improved self-esteem"27

They go on to explain the effects of holding a grudge:

"You might,

- Bring anger and bitterness into every relationship and new experience
- Become so wrapped up in the wrong that you can't enjoy the present
- Become depressed or anxious
- Feel that your life lacks meaning or purpose, or that you're at odds with your spiritual beliefs
- Lose valuable and enriching connectedness with others"[28]
- Is there anything else that can lead me to forgiveness?

Knowing your Abusers Story

I understand that talking with your abuser may not be something you may ever see yourself doing, or it may be impossible for many reasons. I thought it may be helpful for you to hear my story to help you understand another angle that also assisted in the forgiveness process.

27   Mayo Clinic Staff, "Why Is It So Easy to Hold a Grudge?"
28   Mayo Clinic Staff.

I had a list of questions for Bob and his new wife and quickly learned he had told her about the abuse. They had both actually agreed to forgive each other for their past mistakes and do their best to move forward in their new marriage. I was shocked, something I could never see myself being able to do. I then told them of my concerns for their little girl, and his new wife didn't seem too concerned at all, and Bob promised it would never happen again. There was nothing more that I could do, I had at least verbalized my fear and concern.

I then remember asking him, "What are you doing every day of your life to make sure this never happens again?" I was shocked by his response. He said, "This is something I will struggle with for the rest of my life, I'm not going to pretend it will just go away." He then listed the things he does daily to get rid of the yuck in his head and onto a path to healing himself.

I then asked, "What do you think led to the abuse?" Again, very honestly, he admitted to being introduced to pornography at a very young age and becoming addicted. He explained that he could see now that pornography was the catalyst for many poor decisions he made throughout his life, ending with the abuse.

He went on to answer all of the questions I had, very honestly. Some of it was not what I wanted to hear, but I was so impressed that he wasn't just saying things to fool me and make me feel like he was perfectly fine. That was the first day I felt for myself that he was really sorry and wanted to change. After the meeting and understanding Bob's childhood more, I began feeling empathy and compassion for him. There had been people in his life who had hurt him as well, and because he had chosen not to deal with it, the cycle continued. I was grateful to see he was dealing with it now.

I understand that many of you may not ever get to hear your abuser admit to the abuse or feel sorrow for the damage they have caused. Although it does make the process of forgiveness easier, it does not make it impossible to let go. Remember, forgiveness is for your peace of mind and happiness. It is a gift you choose to give yourself.

Forgiveness Activity

This activity is for you to do as many times as needed ONCE you are READY. About two years ago I was introduced to this forgiveness activity by my close friend and life coach, Kimberly Watts. I had no idea I still had issues of forgiveness related to the abuse. It wasn't with my perpetrator, but more with others indirectly in-volved and other issues I had not dealt with over the years. I realized practicing forgiveness is something we need to do every single day. It is a process, and some things take longer than others, and that is ok. Are you ready?

Write the following questions and answers in your journal. Take some time to reflect...

1- Am I holding on to grudges from the past? Make a list...
2- Who do I need to forgive? (and that can include yourself)

Make a list...

Go through your list of persons you need to forgive one at a time. Close your eyes and think about that person and say the following phrases to them in your mind:

1- _____ I Love You
2- _____ I am Sorry
3- _____ Please Forgive Me
4- _____ Thank You

(This is a powerful technique called Ho'oponopono.29)

This technique can truly be life changing, but if you are like me you are thinking, *I love you?? No, I don't. For what? Destroying my life? I am sorry? For what? You hurt me! You're the one that should be sorry! etc.* Hang tight, continue reading, this is powerful!

#1 Say, "I love you because" and explain why you love them... (I am grateful your choices have caused me to reflect and start down a path of becoming a better per-son).

#2 Say, "I am sorry for being so judgmental and not understanding your past..."

#3 Say, "Please forgive me for (hating you for so long, wishing you were dead, etc.)"

#4. Say, "Thank you for helping me to become my best self, for causing me to be more aware of others' difficulties and challenges..."

29   Beauchemin, "Understanding Ho'oponopono."

Expand upon each one as it fits into your situation. Re-peat these over and over again for each person. If you don't feel that way, write it anyway. Just like the truths and lies activity was extremely painful to do in the be-ginning, it gets easier, and your feelings begin to change as you recognize you can forgive others to help *you* lead a happy life. Recognizing there actually is good in your abuse situation for you, is liberating and powerful!

I can honestly say today that if I was given a chance to go back and take the abuse out of my life, I wouldn't do it!! Never would I do it! Because of what I have learned from it and who I have become in the process. I don't believe there are many other ways I could have learned compassion, love and understanding for EVE-RYONE in this world. I was very judgmental in my younger years, and now I may be one of the most for-giving people around. In every situation I hear of, I catch myself wondering about what that person's child-hood must have been like instead of judging, or assuming that they must have been through some very difficult things to be where they are today. That view of the world is so much nicer.

CHAPTER 6

FINDING JOY IN EVERY DAY

I f you are like I was, a few years after the abuse, joy wasn't even a word I recognized anymore. I had for-gotten what happiness felt like and I was too busy just trying to survive without breaking down into tears of frustration and anger to think about being happy. I wish I had known then, the things I know now (I'm going to show you here), because it would have made that time of getting through so much easier.

This last Christmas I took part in a challenge of focusing on something I was grateful for every single day and making a post on social media. I had no idea the difference it would make just in my daily feelings of happiness and joy. As I thought about what I was grateful for and formulated the post each morning, everything negative seemed to escape my mind. I found myself thinking about all of the things I was grateful for throughout the day so I would be prepared for the following day's post. There was so much good that I recognized I had to open up my phone and make a physical list so I wouldn't forget. It was beautiful! I actually continued this challenge long after it ended just because of the difference it made in the way I felt each day. I loved it and was experiencing just what Willie Nelson quotes, *"When I started counting my blessings, my whole life turned around.*" So, I began practicing gratitude every single day and incorporated it into an activity I had previously learned from Life Coach Kimberly Watts.

Gratitude Activity

1. Write a list of 10 of your favorite things or people.
2. Write next to each "why" they are your favorite.
3. Go through your list one at a time and practice gratitude for each.
4. Recognize all of the good in your life right now.
5. Write how you felt as you were focusing on what you are grateful for.
6. Repeat every day for the next couple of weeks.
7. Evaluate your life. Have you felt more joy and happiness?

Try this and pay attention to how you feel. Write down your 10 favorite people or things in your life right now. They can be big things or tiny things. It doesn't matter. Then, write next to each "why" they are your favorite. What do they do or bring to your life that make them your favorite?

Next, go through each one at a time and practice gratitude for those persons or things in your life. For example: Sara is one of my favorite people because she always remembers to check in on me. She listens no matter what I have to say. She always has a smile and brings out the best in me. Another example: The Journey to Heal book is one of my favorite things right now because it opens up my mind to things I never considered before. It has helped me to realize I am not alone in feeling the way I do, and that healing is a process that may take time. It helps me to forgive myself for feeling like I am not ready to forgive my abuser yet.

When you are done writing about each one, take time to recognize that you do have good in your life and pushing through the pain of healing will be worth it. Next, write down how you felt as you were writing about everything you are grateful for. How did you feel inside? Did you feel a glimpse of joy? I encourage you to do this every day for the next couple of weeks and then evaluate your life. Have you felt more joy? Do this activity as often as needed. The more consistent you are the greater the benefits you will notice. I absolutely loved what it did for me. It brought happiness I could not find on my own and it continues to do that each time I do the exercise.

Sultan's Seven Secrets

About a year ago I came to realize I was struggling again with a lot of worthless feelings and negativity inside my head. This had happened many times previous but what a blessing that this time I was able to recognize it early and begin looking for solutions. Not long after, I was introduced to a man named Jeff Beuhner and his book Sultan's Seven Secrets.30 If I could sum up his book in one sentence it would be, *whatever you are thinking and feeling, life will bring you more of it*. He teaches his experience as well as tactics he has shared to help others create whatever they want in their lives. I have to admit at first, I thought his ideas sounded a little out there, but I had heard from so many others how amazing and life-changing his book was so one day I sat down to read it. I couldn't put it down. It totally resonated with me. I completely agreed with what he was explaining and knew I had to put his words into action.

30   Buehner, *The Sultan's Seven Secrets*.

I tried but failed to be consistent enough to really see change and make new habits. I was then invited to a conference to hear him speak. He shared his experience with the story and how he came to write a book. He expanded on what the tactics did for him in his life and I was shocked. I had to make myself stick to practicing what he was teaching for at least a month. Again, I tried but failed trying to do it on my own.

A couple of months went by and a good friend of mine called and said Jeff was doing an online conference for 6 weeks and she was signing up. Because I had tried and failed twice on my own, to carry his tactics through into creating new habits, I knew I had to give this a shot. Boy, am I glad I did! The power of what he had to offer was life-changing!! It was exactly what I needed to clear out the negativity and watch blessings and goodness start to flow into my life. We met with Jeff weekly on a zoom conference call, and he would teach us about a concept, how it would work, what we needed to do to implement it, and then he would give us an assignment to do until we met again the following week. My entire outlook on life was altered. As I began to seriously put his practices to work, the happiness and excitement I felt every day was tangible. My future became exciting, and I couldn't wait for all of the good I knew would be in it. It was at this time that I knew I had to share Jeff's book and course with each of you reading this book and seeking healing and happiness. His tactics work for any dimension in our lives that we want to change.

Ask yourself these questions to find out if Jeff's book, tactics and course are right for you:

Do you focus more on the positive than the negative?
Does your future excite you?
Do you know what you want your future to look like?
Do you know how to get there?
Do you know how to attract positivity?
Do you know how to create a future that not even you would recognize?

If you answered *no* to any of the above questions, I would highly recommend you consider at least reading Jeff's book. This is what his book and course are all about. He also offers a one-week challenge where you can get a taste of him and his work to help you decide if this is right for you. Wait until you hear his story and the stories of so many others who have taken him seriously. I am one of those people. Those things that were once again haunting my life have been removed, and what I am doing now with writing this book and hoping to make a difference for other women, all came from his course. I am so excited about my future and to be doing something worthwhile each and every day. I am full of gratitude for Jeff. My life has become full of purpose.

Tami's Story

One person I will never forget is Tami Iba. She is a mother of 3 beautiful girls and experienced her abuse as a 19-year-old college student.

I met Tami when I was one of the hosts teaching an online challenge to guide women to living holistically healthy lives. Many of the tactics I have shared in this book were what Tami experienced in this online challenge. As she began the course, she was quiet and re-served, but at the end of the month, I didn't even recognize the woman she had become.

At 19 years old Tami was a victim of sexual abuse. She was ridiculed and told it was her fault, so from then on, she hid the abuse. She went on to marry a man she ad-mitted, *"was the best I thought I could do and have,"*31 and for the next 25 years she was mentally and verbally abused by her husband. She eventually mustered the courage to escape the marriage and found the love of her life. Tami had attended PTSD therapy for a year about 12 years into her first marriage when she realized she really needed to address the past. It got her through those few years, but right before we met, she had found herself feeling very lonely and as if she was dying inside again. She stated, *"I would ask myself every day if I even had a purpose."*[32]

For years Tami had accepted and believed that she had no control over her life and often found herself dodging bullets to stay safe and protected. A close friend wanted to help and invited her to an online challenge. Tami felt hope for the first time in a long time, and she saw an opportunity for change. She decided to go 'all in', but the fear and worry of not being able to face the past quickly overcame her. She questioned if this would re-ally work for her and the discomfort of feeling like she was climbing straight up a hill was difficult. Tami did not give up, she was determined, and as time passed, she began feeling tiny changes in her mind and heart.

31   Iba, interview.

32   Iba.

As we provided a safe environment of hope and love in the online challenge, as well as a community of other struggling women, she continued fighting. Shared experiences of abuse and success helped Tami to realize she was not alone, and she started to believe this could really work for her.

When I met Tami, she was fearful and withdrawn. At the beginning of the challenge, she never voiced the in-adequacies she was facing, and she continued to show up every single day. When she finally shared the struggles she had, I realized we had very similar experiences and personalities and I was hopeful this too would work for her. I learned she was not willing to give up and she would do what it was going to take to overcome. And it made a huge difference. She believed in herself again, she was able to rid herself of the daily anger and resentment she was holding onto. Because I saw such incredible results in her I invited her to do the online course with Jeff Beuhner along with me.

Tami stated, *"Before I was introduced to the online challenge and Jeff's six-week course, I felt I had zero control of my life. I had just accepted that. I learned that*

I was living many lies and now I am strong and powerful! I had no idea how much power was sitting inside of me. It is completely up to me to choose what my future is going to look like and become!" [33]

Tami continues, *"I am positive and happy all day every day and I am not the same person I was 6 months ago. Once in a while, I feel some negativity trying to sneak back in and thankfully, I learned how to quickly address it and get rid of it. My life has become amazing, and my future is so bright! Since Jeff's course, I am now helping other women my age to recognize that they too have a purpose and together we can make a difference."* [34]

Isn't that beautiful? Could you feel her entire demeanor change? That is exactly what this book and the activities I have shared can do for you as well, if taken seriously and done consistently. If you are ready to move beyond that or add upon what you learn and feel here, Jeff's book and course are the perfect next step. The link to his book and course is on my Facebook pages.

33   Iba.
34   Iba

CHAPTER 7

PROFESSIONAL THERAPY

I would never advise anyone to try and reach healing alone. All of the tactics I have shared have changed my life in so many ways and have become daily processes for overcoming various other issues as well, but it would be silly of me to not recommend therapy. It saved my life!!

Dr. David Spiegel, M.D., associate chair of Psychiatry and Behavioral Sciences at Stanford University teaches, *"A professional can help you dissect a problem -- then help you figure out how to solve it. Just as a life coach can help you formulate a plan to make a significant change in your life, therapy can help you develop a strategy to handle a current hardship you may be facing. Spiegel says that speaking with a professional allows you to look at any hill you're climbing from a new angle."*[35]

Professionals are ready to help you in ways this book and tactics cannot. Some things just have to be dealt with on a professional therapeutic level to be permanently left in the past. For this reason, I would highly recommend professional therapy to every childhood sexual abuse survivor. Therapists will guide you in your specific journey and will be able to see how to direct you the entire way, step by step. And please never for-get, trying a different therapist until you find the perfect fit for you is completely necessary and essential to your healing. This is normal to therapists, and most encourage you to shop around.

Furthermore, attending therapy in various stages of your life, as a childhood sexual abuse survivor, is very important. Like I shared, after my childhood experience with therapy, I went many years thinking I was completely fine. Thank goodness others convinced me that I may be over the abuse and had forgiven my abuser, but there were many aftereffects they were seeing that could also be addressed and overcome with the help of a therapist.

35   Holmes, "4 Ways Everyone Can Benefit From Therapy."

How do I identify aftereffects I may be dealing with?

Let's do one last activity. Write down all of the things you feel you would like to improve about yourself that may or may not have anything to do with the abuse. Here was my list:

1.   Depression
2.   Anxiety
3.   Irritability
4.   Easily Angered/Anger Issues
5.   Judgmental
6.   Eating Disorder
7.   Body Image Issues
8.   Perfectionism
9.   Ignoring Problems
10. Impatience
11. Isolation
12. Comparing Myself to Others
13. Never Feeling Like I am Enough
14. Negativity
15. Short Tempered
16. Others may include:
17. Alcoholism

18. Drug Abuse
19. Harming Yourself
20. Shoplifting
21. Lying
22. Unhealthy Sexual Relationships
23. Hurting Others

Do any of those sound familiar? Remember, it is so important for you to be honest with yourself. This is only going to help you become better. The first step is recognition.

The list I gave above, I had been dealing with for years and never connected the behaviors as aftereffects of the abuse. There are so many behaviors that are connected with childhood trauma, and the list above is just scratching the surface. So, if you come up with others not on my list, they are most likely aftereffects of the trauma you endured in one way or another. And let's be honest, does it really matter where the behavior came from? The important part is the recognition, desire for change, and willingness to seek for help to overcome.

Once Mrs. Kimberly Watts and others pointed out that my behaviors were most likely aftereffects of the abuse, I honestly was relieved to recognize where the issues had come from. I couldn't understand why others seemed to have it all together and I was such a mess. I then knew I needed to do some more work on healing. So, I called and found a therapist near my home. Once I was there, it felt so good, and I was so excited to get rid of all of the yuck!

I'm sure this second bout at therapy will not be the last and I will continue to need more professional guidance in my future. I am so grateful for those around me who have cared about me enough to help me see that I needed more direction. I'm also equally as grateful to have so many tools in my tool belt (that I have shared with you in this book) to use on a daily basis to keep me improving and at least at status quo. I now know that as soon as those tools are not working, I need additional professional help.

So, what do you do with your list? I encourage you to first work on what is causing you the most pain or havoc in your life. If it is anger and resentment towards your perpetrator, start there. If you feel you are over that, consider what is troubling you most and begin there. Remember, everything takes time, and you are not on a time constraint!! Do your best each day, be as consistent as possible with the tools given in this book and with the direction of a therapist, and as you are able to see improvements, move on to the next item of business. Happy Healing!

For additional assistance with understanding and applying each of the tools outlined in this book, I invite you to join me and listen in to my podcast entitled *It Was Not Your Fault*. You can also interact with other child-hood sexual abuse survivors working towards healing in my private Facebook group Support & Healing from the aftereffects of Childhood Sexual Abuse.

BIBLIOGRAPHY

Archuleta, David. I Will Go and Do. Online Video, 2019. https://www.youtube.com/watch?v=zeGC8lS20 d8.

Asheville Ward News. "Asheville Ward News." Accessed May 5, 2021. https://ashevillewardnews.com/.

Beauchemin, Molly. "Understanding Ho'oponopono: A Beautiful Hawaiian Prayer for Forgiveness." Grace & Lightness Magazine (blog), June 26, 2020. https://graceandlightness.com/hooponopono-hawaiian-prayer-for-forgiveness/.

Buehner, Jeff. The Sultan's Seven Secrets, 2020. https://books.apple.com/us/book/the-sultans-seven-secrets/id1523550447.

Carty, Carolyn Joyce. "Footprints in the Sand." In Footprints in the Sand: One Night a Man Had a Dream, by Carolyn Joyce Carty, Ella H. Scharring-Hausen, and Robert Louis Scharring-Hausen, 77. Authorhouse / Footprints Publishings Inc, 2004.

Clear, James. Atomic Habits: An Easy & Proven Way to Build Good Habits & Break Bad Ones. New York: Avery, 2018.
Daigle, Lauren. You Say (Official Music Video). Online Video, 2018. https://www.youtube.com/watch?v=sIaT8Jl2zpI.

Eyring, Henry B. "Adversity." The Church of Jesus Christ of Latter-Day Saints (blog), April 2009. https://www.churchofjesuschrist.org/study/general-conference/2009/04/adversity?lang=eng.

"Tested, Proved, and Polished." The Church of Jesus Christ

of Latter-Day Saints (blog), October 20, 2005. https://www.churchofjesuschrist.org/study/general-conference/2020/10/51eyring?lang=eng.

Holmes, Lindsay. "4 Ways Everyone Can Benefit from Therapy." HuffPost (blog), August 7, 2014. https://www.huffpost.com/entry/benefits-of-therapy-and-life-coaches_n_5635389.

Iba, Tami. Interview by Lindsey Preece. Phone, October 23, 2020. Kimberly Watts. "True Behavioral Change (Graph)," 2021.

MacKenzie, Jackson. Psychopath Free: Recovering from Emotionally Abusive Relationships with Narcissists, Sociopaths, and Other Toxic People. Expanded edition. Berkley, 2015.

Mayo Clinic Staff. "Why Is It So Easy to Hold a Grudge?" Mayo Clinic, November 13, 2020. https://www.mayoclinic.org/healthy-lifestyle/adult-health/in-depth/forgiveness/art-20047692.

Smith, Joseph. The Book of Mormon: Another Testament of Jesus Christ. Translation edition. New York: Harmony, 2006.

Smith, Joseph, and Oliver Cowdery. The Doctrine and Covenants of the Church of Jesus Christ of Latter Day Saints: Carefully Selected from the Revelations of God. Salt Lake City, UT: Church of Jesus Christ of Latter-Day Saints, 2020.

Sutherland, Crystal M. Journey to Heal: Seven Essential Steps of Recovery for Survivors of Childhood Sexual Abuse. Kregel Publications, 2016.

Theo, Harrison. "The Five Stages of Grief: Exploring The Kübler-Ross Model." Mind Journal (blog), July 8, 2020. https://themindsjournal.com/kubler-ross-model-grief/.

AUTHOR'S BIOGRAPHY

Lindsey Lish Preece is a mother, Registered Nurse, International Speaker, Author, Full-time Coach and Mentor for victims of past various traumas. As a survivor of childhood sexual abuse herself, she has become passionate about guiding others along their path to healing, overcoming negative after effects, and living an abundantly joyful life after life-altering events. Lindsey is not a therapist. She shares her 30 year journey of healing and what finally led to self-confidence, self-love, inner peace and FREEDOM from it all! More of her work and support, including Coaching, can be found on her website: www.pain-to-purpose.com, private Facebook Group: Christian Women Transforming Pain into Purpose (Mind, Body & Spirit) with HIM, and Facebook: Lindsey Lish Preece.

WORKBOOK

It Was Not Your Fault:
How to Overcome the Negative Effects
of Childhood Sexual Abuse

Chapter II: Stages of Healing (Grief)

Acknowledging and Accepting the Abuse Exercise

You might find this part painful, and that is not only ok, but expected. Take your time to get through each exercise, it is not a race. Remember, the outcome will be so worth it!

Step by Step

1. Start by writing all the details of your story as you know them to be true. Write EVERYTHING, leaving nothing out. Here are a couple of questions from the Journey to Heal author that helped me and can help you write your story as well:

How old were you when the abuse began?

Who was involved?

What happened?

Was it a one-time event, or was it repeated over time?

Write until you cannot remember anything more.

2. Read back through what you have written, consciously accepting the details as part of your story.
3. Burn it, rip it up, or save it.

You did it! How do you feel? If you feel some relief, great! If you feel terrible, that is great too! You are working through the pain so you can let it go. You may have to repeat this more than once to get the desired effect. Major change will not happen overnight, but you will notice subtle changes right away. Don't stop! You are on your way to a bright and beautiful future. Trust me.

Releasing Anger Exercise

Here are a few writing exercises that worked miracles for me! I also learned this one from the book, Journey to Heal. It is intended to help you begin dealing with and releasing the ineffective anger.

Step by Step

1. Acknowledge and accept that you have anger.

First step, acknowledge the anger. Accept that you have anger or repressed anger that needs to be released. If you are not sure if you have anger to release, ask someone close to you if they see anger in you or feel you are holding onto anger. Be prepared to accept what they tell you and remember, you asked them. They just want to help you.

2. Next, ask yourself: If I could identify one thing about the abuse that hurts the most, what would it be?

Does it have to do with your abuser, or someone indirectly involved, or with the abuse itself? (Example of someone indirectly involved would be: You confided in your aunt and she didn't believe you or said you were lying or making it up for attention, and now you are angry with her.)

3. Fill out this sentence with each person identified:

— I am angry with _____ because of _____

_____

_____.

— I am angry with _____ because of _____

_____

_____.

— I am angry with _____ because of _____

_____

_____.

— I am angry with _____ because of _____

_____

_____.

— I am angry with _____ because of _____

_____

_____.

— I am angry with _____ because of _____

_____

_____.

— I am angry with _____ because of _____

_____

_____.

4. Take each sentence you wrote in the last exercise and expand upon them. Write everything that is weighing you down or causing you feelings of anger about that person. Don't stop writing until you can't think of anything more. Do this for each person.

_____

_____

_____

_____

_____

_____

_____

_____

_____

_____

_____

_____

It Was Not Your Fault

5. Take each of those sentences you have expanded upon and write a letter to the person you have anger towards. Include all the details of how you feel and how that person has negatively affected your life. Be honest, get all real feelings out of your head and onto paper. Write all the things that you would say if you had the courage to say them.

You can write the letters in this workbook or on a separate paper, depending on what you plan to do with the letter when it is done.

_____

_____

_____

_____

_____

_____

_____

_____

_____

_____

_____

_____

_____

_____

_____

_____

_____

_____

_____

_____

_____

_____

It Was Not Your Fault

_____

_____

_____

_____

_____

_____

_____

_____

_____

_____

_____

_____

_____

| It Was Not Your Fault

It Was Not Your Fault

| It Was Not Your Fault

_____

_____

_____

_____

_____

_____

_____

_____

_____

_____

_____

_____

It Was Not Your Fault

6. Take the letter/letters and rip it up, burn it, hide it, or send it.

I challenge you, for the next week, each time you feel any type of anger, take out a paper or type up a letter expressing all of your feelings without holding back. Do it over and over and over again and then decide what you want to do with them each time you are finished.

Then, at the end of the week evaluate how you feel. Write your feelings here: (I would also love to hear from you on my private facebook page *Support & Healing from the after effects of Childhood Sexual Abuse* about what this exercise did for you. This is a wonderful opportunity to share your feelings and encourage others to do the exercises found in this book).

_____

_____

_____

_____

_____

_____

_____

_____

_____

It Was Not Your Fault

Chapter III: Understanding and Believing IT WAS NOT YOUR FAULT!

How to Achieve True Behavioral Change Exercise

1. Ask yourself, what is a behavior I want to change? (Examples: anger, self-hate, self-harm, substance abuse, rage, compulsive spending, comfort eating or starving yourself, negativity, irritability, physically/emotionally abusing someone else, etc.)

_____

_____

_____

_____

2. Identify the lies you are living that may be contributing to this behavior. Ask yourself, what are my deepest thoughts when I am involved in this behavior? What feelings am I trying to cover up or deal with? (Examples: I am worthless, No one will ever want me, I should have prevented the abuse, I wish I wouldn't have..., I wish I could cause my abuser pain, I hate my abuser f or ruining my life, Why, did God let this happen to me? Etc.)

Thoughts:

_____

_____

_____

_____

_____

_____

_____

_____

_____

_____

_____

Examples:

Thought: *I am worthless.*

Lie: The abuse has ruined me. I'm not deserving of anything good.

Thought: *No one will ever want me.*

Lie: The abuse has ruined me. I'm not deserving of a good person in my life.

Thought: *I should have prevented the abuse.*

Lie: The abuse was my fault.

Thought: *I wish I wouldn't have....*

Lie: The abuse was my fault.

Thought: *I wish I could cause my abuser pain.*

Lie: It is my job to make sure my abuser pays for the abuse.

Thought: *I hate my abuser for ruining my life.*

Lie: My life is ruined because of the abuse.

Thought: *Why did God let this happen to me?*

Lie: God does not love me. God is punishing me for...

Thought: *I cannot believe someone could do something so disgusting.*

Lie: I will never forgive my abuser.

Take the list of repetitive thoughts above and state the lies you are living and telling yourself in combination with these thoughts.

List your lies:

Lie #1: _____

Lie #2: _____

Lie #3: _____

Lie #4: _____

Lie #5: _____

Lie #6: _____

Lie #7: _____

Lie #8: _____

1. Take each lie from above and turn it into a truth by writing the opposite, even if you do not believe it!!

Examples:

Lie: I'm not deserving of anything good.

Truth: Whomever I marry will be so lucky. I can become anything I want to become.

Lie: The abuse was my fault.

Truth: The abuse had nothing to do with me, and it was absolutely not my fault.

Lie: It is my job to make sure my abuser pays for the abuse.

Truth: It is not my job to punish my abuser, I will focus on my happiness alone.

Lie: My life is ruined because of the abuse.

Truth: I am powerful, the abuse will make me a better and stronger person.

Lie: God does not love me. God is punishing me for...

Truth: God loves me so much that He has allowed an opportunity for me to become more like Him. God will help me every step of the way if I want Him to.

Lie: I will never forgive my abuser. Sexual abuse in unforgivable.

Truth: Forgiveness is for my happiness alone and does not mean I am ok with what happened.

List your truths:

Truth #1_____

Truth #2_____

Truth #3_____

Truth #4_____

Truth #5_____

Truth #6_____

Truth #7_____

Truth #8_____

Extra Tip: If there is anything in your life that you would like to become or believe about yourself this is your opportunity to add it to your truths list. Treat it as any of your other truths.

2. Take this list of truths and keep it next to your bed or posted on your fridge or bathroom mirror and repeat these new truths to yourself out loud every morning and every night at least. Soon you will have them memorized and I encourage you to recite them over and over in your mind throughout the day. It will be difficult at first, especially because you probably won't believe them, but I promise you change is happening and pretty soon it will bring a smile to your face as you recite, and a desire to become those new truths will begin. Pay close attention to your new actions, desires and feelings as you start believing these new truths.

3. Process and Actions: As you begin processing and believing these new truths, you may notice you start to do things you didn't do before. For example, if one of the truths you are reciting is *I can become anything I want to become*, you may find as you continue reciting this daily, your mind may make a shift and you may naturally start feeling lighter, happier, more excited for the future, etc. Continue acting on these new feelings and enjoy every minute of it. This is a new truth you are speaking to yourself.

Also, take the time to come up with some actions you can commit to each day that will help you become whatever it is that you want to become. For example, if you want to become an author, begin down the path of writing your first book. Start brainstorming ideas or researching and asking around to those who can guide you on making this a reality.

If you want to become the best mother in the world, then ask yourself, what would that look like for me? Maybe you came up with: I would listen intently to my children when they talk to me. I will not raise my voice. I will spend 15 minutes a day of uninterrupted time with each child. Now it's time to act on these identified actions. Get excited! True behavioral change will come as you truly believe and take action steps towards these new truths.

List daily action steps you are going to take:

_____

_____

_____

_____

_____

_____

_____

_____

4. The desired outcome will naturally be achieved as you believe these truths and act upon them daily.

Chapter IV: Relationship with God/Higher Power

Inviting God in Exercise

List some things I am willing to try to see if God/Higher Power can help me too:

_____

_____

_____

_____

_____

_____

_____

_____

Chapter V: Forgiveness

Forgiveness Exercise

This activity is for you to do as many times as needed ONCE you are READY.

About two years ago I was introduced to this forgiveness activity by my close friend and life coach, Kimberly Watts. I had no idea I still had issues of forgiveness related to the abuse. It wasn't with my perpetrator, but more with others indirectly involved and other issues I had not dealt with over the years. I realized practicing forgiveness is something we need to do every single day. It is a process, and some things take longer than others, and that is ok. Are you ready?

Write the following questions and answers. Take some time to reflect...
1- Am I holding on to grudges from the past? What are the grudges?

Make a list...

-
-
-
-
-
-
-
-
-

2 Who do I need to forgive? (and that can include yourself)

Make a list...

-
-
-
-
-
-
-
-
-
-
-
-

Go through your list of persons you need to forgive one at a time. Close your eyes and think about that person and say the following phrases to them in your mind:

1- _____ I Love You

2- _____ I am Sorry

3- _____ Please Forgive Me

4- _____Thank You

(This is a powerful technique called Ho'oponopono.)

Example:

#1 Say, "I love you because" and explain why you love them... (I am grateful your choices have caused me to reflect and start down a path of becoming a better person).

#2 Say, "I am sorry for being so judgmental and not understanding your past..."

#3 Say, "Please forgive me for (hating you for so long, wishing you were dead, etc.)"

#4. Say, "Thank you for helping me to become my best self, for causing me to be more aware of others' difficulties and challenges, etc...."

Expand upon each one as it fits into your situation. Repeat these over and over again for each person. If you don't feel that way, write it anyway. Just like the truths and lies activity was extremely painful to do in the beginning, it gets easier, and your feelings begin to change as you recognize you can forgive others to help you lead a happy life. Recognizing there actually is good in your abuse situation for you, is liberating and powerful!

First person: _____

1- _____ I Love You because

_____

_____

_____

2- _____ I am Sorry for

_____

_____

_____

3- _____ Please Forgive Me for _____

_____

_____

_____

4- _____ Thank You for ____

_____

_____

_____

Second person: _____

1- _____ I Love You because

_____

_____

_____

2- _____ I am Sorry for

_____

_____

_____

3- _____Please Forgive Me for ____

_____

_____

_____

4- _____ Thank You for ____

_____

_____

_____

Third person: _____

1- _____ I Love You because

_____

_____

_____

2- _____ I am Sorry for

_____

_____

_____

3- _____Please Forgive Me for _____

_____

_____

_____

4- _____ Thank You for _____

_____

_____

_____

Fourth person: _____

1- _____ I Love You because

_____

_____

_____

2- _____ I am Sorry for

_____

_____

_____

3- _____Please Forgive Me for _____

_____

_____

_____

4- _____ Thank You for _____

_____

_____

_____

Fifth person: _____

1- _____ I Love You because

_____

_____

_____

2- _____ I am Sorry for

_____

_____

_____

3- _____Please Forgive Me for _____

_____

_____

_____

4- _____ Thank You for _____

_____

_____

_____

Six person: _____

1- _____ I Love You because

_____

_____

_____

2- _____ I am Sorry for

_____

_____

_____

3- _____Please Forgive Me for _____

_____

_____

_____

4- _____ Thank You for _____

_____

_____

_____

Chapter VI: Finding Joy in Every Day

Gratitude Exercise

1. Try this and pay attention to how you feel. Write down your 10 favorite people or things in your life right now. They can be big things or tiny things. It doesn't matter.

-
-
-
-
-
-
-
-

2. Then, write next to each "why" they are your favorite. What do they do or bring to your life that makes them your favorite?

For example: Sara is one of my favorite people because she always remembers to check in on me. She listens no matter what I have to say. She always has a smile and brings out the best in me.

Another example: The Journey to Heal book is one of my favorite things right now because it opens up my mind to things I never considered before. It has helped me to realize I am not alone in feeling the way I do, and that healing is a process that may take time. It helps me to forgive myself for feeling like I am not ready to forgive my abuser yet.

Your turn:

- _____
  is my favorite because _____
  _____

- _____
  is my favorite because _____
  _____

- _____
  is my favorite because _____
  _____

- _____
  is my favorite because _____
  _____

- _____
  is my favorite because _____
  _____

- _____
  is my favorite because _____
  _____

- _____
  is my favorite because _____
  _____

- _____
  is my favorite because _____
  _____

- _____
  is my favorite because _____
  _____

- _____
  is my favorite because _____
  _____

3. Next, go through each one at a time and practice gratitude for those persons or things in your life. Recognize that you do have good in your life and pushing through the pain of healing will be worth it.

4. Now, write down how you felt as you were writing about everything you are grateful for. How did you feel inside? Did you feel a glimpse of joy?

_____

_____

_____

_____

_____

_____

_____

_____

_____

_____

5. Continue to do this every day for the next couple of weeks and then evaluate your life. Have you felt more joy and happiness? What has been different?

_____

_____

_____

_____

_____

_____

_____

_____

_____

6. Do this activity as often as needed. The more consistent you are the greater the benefits you will notice. I absolutely loved what it did for me. It brought happiness I could not find on my own and it continues to do that each time I do the exercise.

Chapter VII: Professional Therapy

Where to Start Exercise

Write down all of the things you feel you would like to improve about yourself that may or may not have anything to do with the abuse.

Here was my list:

Depression
Anxiety
Irritability
Easily Angered/Anger Issues
Judgmental
Eating Disorder
Body Image Issues
Perfectionism
Ignoring Problems
Impatience
Isolation
Comparing Myself to Others
Never Feeling Like I am Enough
Negativity
Short Tempered
Others may include:
Alcoholism
Drug Abuse
Harming Yourself
Shoplifting
Lying
Unhealthy Sexual Relationships
Hurting Others

Your list:

-
-
-
-
-
-
-
-
-
-
-
-
-

What do you do with your list?

I encourage you to first work on what is causing you the most pain or havoc in your life. If it is anger and resentment towards your perpetrator, start there. If you feel you are over that, consider what is troubling you most and begin there.

Remember, everything takes time, and you are not on a time constraint!! Do your best each day, be as consistent as possible with the tools given in this book and with the direction of a therapist, and as you are able to see improvements, move onto the next item of business. Happy Healing!

For additional assistance with understanding and applying each of the tools outlined in this book, I invite you to join me on Facebook in my Private FB Group *Christian Women Transforming Pain into Purpose (Mind, Body, & Spirit) with HIM* at this link: https://www.facebook.com/groups/3507211369560971/. You can also inquire about my Coaching Program here: https://www.pain-to-purpose.com/